RUST
IN PEACE

ALSO BY DAVE MUSTAINE

Mustaine: A Heavy Metal Memoir

RUST IN PEACE

THE INSIDE STORY OF THE MEGADETH MASTERPIECE

DAVE MUSTAINE
with JOEL SELVIN

hachette
BOOKS

NEW YORK

Hachette Books
Hachette Book Group
1290 Avenue of the Americas
New York, NY 10104
HachetteBooks.com
Twitter.com/HachetteBooks
Instagram.com/HachetteBooks

First Edition: September 2020

Hachette Books is a division of Hachette Book Group, Inc.
The Hachette Books name and logo are trademarks of Hachette Book Group, Inc.

The publisher is not responsible for websites (or their content) that are not
owned by the publisher.

The Hachette Speakers Bureau provides a wide range of authors for speaking
events. To find out more, go to www.hachettespeakersbureau.com or call
(866) 376-6591.

Print book interior design by Linda Mark.

Library of Congress Cataloging-in-Publication Data has been applied for.
ISBNs: 978-0-306-84602-1 (hardcover); 978-0-306-84603-8 (e-book)

Printed in the United States of America
LSC-C

10 9 8 7 6 5 4 3 2 1

Dedicated to all my fans around the globe

Aguante Megadeth!

CONTENTS

FOREWORD BY SLASH

As told to Ryan J. Downey

THERE WAS THIS WHOLE UNDERGROUND METAL THING happening in the early '80s, with a handful of bands circulating demos and appearing on indie compilations. It was a small scene, but the people who knew about it went nuts over it. I knew about Metallica back then, before they had a record deal, but I didn't actually meet those guys for a few more years.

I have no idea about the dynamics or details that led to the split between Dave Mustaine and Metallica, but all things considered, it was meant to be. We are all better off for it. Because otherwise, we wouldn't have had the focus on Dave that came with him leading his own band.

We wouldn't have had Megadeth.

Steven Adler and I loved *Peace Sells . . . But Who's Buying?* It was our favorite record. I was in love with everything about the album, but I liked the guitar playing especially, of course. Chris

Poland remains, to this day, one of my favorite lead guitar players that Dave has had in Megadeth.

Guns N' Roses was kind of laying low, in a holding pattern, around that time. We had become a pretty well-known band in LA, but after we signed with Geffen Records, we went sort of under the radar for a while. The record company didn't want us doing many gigs around then.

I could be wrong, but I think it was Steven who introduced me to David Ellefson. Junior is a very sincere, friendly, and outgoing person. There are no airs with him. Mustaine was a bit more serious, much more sort of reserved socially, but we all got along really well together.

Steven and Izzy Stradlin were renting this, like, "guest house" just south of Sunset. I was hanging out at some chick's place; I didn't actually live anywhere, technically. Mustaine had an apartment just around the corner from where I was staying, maybe a couple of blocks away.

I started hanging around over there a lot and became really good friends with Junior and Dave. We did a lot of partying, but it wasn't "partying" in the traditional sense. We weren't at the bar. In fact, "partying" isn't even really the right word, as far as what that connotates for most people. It's quite the opposite, actually. It was very insular. We stayed inside, did drugs, and made music. We jammed quite a bit. We wrote some pretty dark, heavy, drug-fueled shit together.

I never became a metal guy, but I related to something about the way both Dave Mustaine and James Hetfield approached guitar. There were a lot of thrash bands, but those two created a sound unique unto themselves. There are bits and pieces in my playing that came from listening to those guys and especially from jamming with Dave. It definitely had some influence on me. I really dug playing with him. I'm a riff guy and he has a certain way of riffing that appeals to me.

Dave's style of guitar playing is so uniquely his own; it's difficult to put into words. His fingering style, his overall approach. It's instantly recognizable. I know it's him, immediately.

I talked about this a little bit in my book, but there was a point when all of us were temporarily frustrated with our existing bands and so we briefly talked about maybe teaming up together, 'though we never pursued it in earnest. I loved Megadeth, but my heart was in Guns.

Guns made *Appetite* with producer Mike Clink. Not long before we geared up to go back into the studio to make the *Use Your Illusion* records, Mike told me he was working with Megadeth. "How's it going?" I'd ask. "What are you guys doing?" He'd share anecdotal info, like, they'd just finished vocals, or they were doing overdubs, but I didn't have many details.

Then I heard the record.

Rust in Peace is a great album.

It's a great *sounding* album, too.

I'm a pretty big Megadeth fan. I can't think of a Megadeth album that I would consider "not worthy." There's something cool and memorable on pretty much every record. *Peace Sells . . .* was clearly a milestone for them, but *Rust in Peace* put the band on the map on a bigger scale. It broadened their audience. It made Megadeth a household name, by metal standards. It has really fucking cool songs on it. "Hangar 18" is awesome. Marty Friedman is great, obviously. I mean, there's just a bunch of cool shit on that record. I certainly understand why every important *Rust in Peace* anniversary is celebrated as a pivotal moment for both Megadeth and for heavy metal.

ACKNOWLEDGMENTS

OR NEARLY THIRTY YEARS, I HAVE BEEN PROUDLY LIS-tening to fans and music critics alike proclaim that *Rust in Peace* is one of the greatest and most influential metal records of all time, and it's truly one of my proudest offerings. I hope to retell the tale of the writing, recording, and simply living, if you can call it that, of the *Rust in Peace* years. Once you start reading this, you will see why the recording was so explosive and volatile, and when you finish this, hopefully, you will understand me and Megadeth just a little bit better; just like I do now.

I'm glad I took this trip back down memory lane. I remember a lot from that period of recording *RIP*, with all the drama, but this is even more detailed, more painful, more rewarding, more revealing, and more exciting when hearing all the missing parts, and all the others' perspectives during that time. I sincerely thank all those who contributed to this as well.

Deep thanks go to my amazing manager, Cory Brennan, and 5B Artist Management, especially Chris Shields, Bob Johnsen,

ACKNOWLEDGMENTS

and Justin Arcangel. I'd like to also thank Zora Ellis and Stephen Reeder. Oh, how I wish 5BAM had been managing Megadeth from the start.

This amazing tale was captured and told by wordsmith Joel Selvin. And of course, thank you to Ben Schafer, Fred Francis, Carrie Napolitano, Amanda Kain, Michael Barrs, and Anna Hall of Hachette Books for helping me give another compelling look deep into the unknown of Dave Mustaine and the Megadeth saga.

I'd like to thank my excellent wife, Pam, who is constantly pushing me to be my best, our outstanding children, Justis (my best friend) and Electra Mustaine, for loving me when I fall and always encouraging me to get up. Thank you to our webmaster, friend, and CyberArmy Fanclub President, Dave McRobb.

Obvious thanks go to the *Rust in Peace* lineup: Marty Friedman, David Ellefson, and Nick Menza. I must also thank the other members of this story: Andy Sommers, Mike Clink, Micajah Ryan, Max Norman, Tony Lettieri, Randy Kertz, and Bob Nalbandian.

Finally, it's with deep gratitude that I thank the former players for Megadeth.

Last, but not least . . . thank you, Vic.

DAVE MUSTAINE

Hey, Slash!

I wanna thank you for all the cool times we chilled, albeit briefly, either jamming or hanging out with Jr. and the other band guys . . . or whoever was at one of our apartments at any given moment.

I hope you know how much I dug those times. Hell, I still remember sitting on the couch, next to a pet boa constrictor or python you owned, watching in total amazement as you effortlessly shredded your guitar with solo after solo.

So, beloved brother, it was a "no-brainer" asking you to do the foreword for my second book, and I was pumped when you said yes! I give enormous thanks to you for writing the foreword to this new book! I just can't think of a cooler person to have done this. In other words: Thanks, Fucking Dude! You Fucking Rock, Man!

Dave Mustaine

- ONE -

CASTLE DONINGTON

B EGINNINGS CAN OFTEN BE FOUND INSIDE ENDINGS. This story begins at an ending, the Megadeth performance August 20, 1988, at the Monsters of Rock festival at Castle Donington, where the band was to appear before a record crowd of 108,000, playing through a more than 100,000-watt sound system—so large it made the *Guinness Book of World Records*—on a bill with Iron Maiden, Kiss, David Lee Roth, and a new band from Los Angeles whose first album, *Appetite for Destruction*, was starting to make some noise back in the States.

DAVE MUSTAINE: Everybody was strung out and, of course, you never take enough heroin, so everybody ran out and got dope sick. Our bassist, David Ellefson—we called him Junior to avoid having a second Dave in the band—couldn't handle it. He snapped. He told our manager that he was a junkie. Everybody had known about my bad habits, but not about David's. They came up with this lie that he fell in the tub and sprained his wrist, but he never did.

At Castle Donington, the show went off, but what happened after was the beginning of things falling apart. We had just finished the Iron Maiden Seventh Son of a Seventh Son tour in America, and I thought that had been a great opportunity for us. After Donington, we had another seven stadium dates as support to Iron Maiden through Europe. *So Far So Good . . . So What!,* our third album, had come out in January, and we had just done the video for "In My Darkest Hour" for the Penelope Spheeris movie *The Decline of Western Civilization.*

CHUCK BEHLER: I was only the drummer in the band for less than two years. We went from clubs to arenas that quick. To play a show like Donington was just unimaginable to me, and we were excited. We had already done America, Europe, and Japan and took a little break. I was really looking forward to this show because I had the album *Monsters of Rock* from the first festival in 1980, with Ritchie Blackmore's Rainbow and the other bands. The cover of the record featured a live overhead shot of this massive crowd. I knew there were going to be a lot of people. I was kind of nervous, but at the same time I was really looking forward to that.

DAVID ELLEFSON: I had the same Castle Donington record as a kid growing up in Minnesota; Rainbow, Quiet Riot, Scorpions, April Wine—cool bands that I was into. It was this mythical, legendary festival that still maintained its stature as the *crème de la crème* of all European rock festivals. As an American metal band, the goal was always to break in Europe—that was really the end game—because once you broke in Europe, you had planted your flag, you were deemed cool, worthy. Of course, Metallica had a huge leg up on that, drummer Lars Ulrich being from Denmark. He knew how to connect with that. But Anthrax had also been there. Slayer had been over there. Megadeth had gone over only a couple of times, so this was really a huge moment for us. But Metallica had certainly broken down a lot of doors before all of us.

We played a warmup for the show at the Ritz in New York. We were going to fly to New York, play the Ritz, and from there, fly over to England, which was good because it gave us one last chance to cop and make sure we had enough drugs to get from New York to England. None of us smuggled heroin. We never brought drugs through borders or any of that stuff. By the time we got to England and were driving up to Donington, some of us were coming down off the heroin and starting to jones. I was thinking Guns N' Roses was going to be there, and we knew they got high. We knew that they were like us; they did heroin and coke.

CHUCK BEHLER: We stayed in an old-style hotel where Guns N' Roses was staying too. I hung out a lot with their drummer, Steven Adler, a cool guy. He told me, "This is it—this is the gig, man. It doesn't get any better than this." He was kind of nervous. We got on the bus to go to the gig and when we drove past the fence and saw the crowd for the first time, it was almost overwhelming. It was a sea of people. We had done a sound check the day before—there were so many bands, they held sound checks for three days before the festival; we did ours the same day as Kiss and Guns N' Roses—but nobody was there. The day of the show, though, it was just . . . wow.

DAVE MUSTAINE: At the hotel the night before Castle Donington, the bar was a who's who of hard rock. The promoter showed up in his Lamborghini Countach to check on everybody. This was his biggest show ever. We weren't the only band jonesing for heroin. Someone said one of the Guns N' Roses guys got mugged out in the streets that night trying to score.

DAVID ELLEFSON: Heroin is a very difficult drug to tour with. Whereas coke, pot, and beer were readily available, heroin was not. Guns N' Roses had just come off a huge run though America with Aerosmith and they were mostly cleaned up. We were not. We stayed at a hotel at Leicester Square, and the Iron Maiden guys were there. In addition to being super jet-lagged, I was coming down hard off my heroin. I was getting dope sick big-time. My girlfriend Charlie was with me, and she had put her foot down about the drugs when we first got together, so I had been hiding my habit from her. And everybody else but Dave. But now the word was out.

I called a doctor to come to the hotel, and he wrote me a prescription for codeine, which, when you're on heroin, is like taking baby aspirin. It doesn't really do much. The doctor was disgusted with me and called me a "fucking American drug addict." Our agent, Andy Somers, was there and he chastised me, telling me how disappointed in me he was. The whole fucking house of cards was crumbling down.

That night, Charlie got extravagantly drunk. The next day when we had to leave to go to Donington Park, she was still so fucked up I had to leave her in my bunk on our bus. She was a wreck. Meanwhile, I was dope sick and felt terrible. Biggest day of my life, biggest day of the band's career, our biggest show ever, and

I'm fucking not fully present because I was so strung out. All of our heroes were there—Iron Maiden, Kiss, David Lee Roth.

DAVE MUSTAINE: His girlfriend was really bad. She was very controlling. She once made him dump a gram of heroin into the carpet. Too bad he didn't know that if you blew up a balloon and rubbed it over the carpet, all the heroin would stick to the balloon and it would come out of the carpet, but he was pretty much an amateur junkie. Ha-ha.

CHUCK BEHLER: I was standing on the side of the stage watching Guns N' Roses with Lars Ulrich, who was there hanging out. We had no idea what was happening, but the band suddenly stopped playing. At first, I just thought it was some weirdness because Guns N' Roses back then was known for doing all kinds of crazy stuff. Stopping playing in the middle of a show was just the kind of crap they would pull. Steven got off his drums and pointed into the audience. I thought maybe vocalist Axl Rose was mad at somebody and had jumped into the crowd. He would do stuff like that. But when the band went silent and walked off the stage, it was obvious something else went wrong. It turned out that the massive crowd, slipping around on a muddy, soggy field, had crushed two people down in front. The kids died, but we didn't know that until much later. We did know they were hurt because we saw the ambulance come. I don't know how the heck they got them out of there, but they did. Dave and I gave an interview between sets to a local radio station and we didn't mention anything, even though it was on our minds.

DAVE MUSTAINE: I was not watching Guns N' Roses when the people got crushed to death, but we were all aware what had happened. There were a lot of people pulled out of the crowd who were getting crushed. It was a terrible setup. The hill sloped down to the stage from the far end of the raceway. The field was sloppy and muddy from rain. With a hundred thousand people at the top of the hill, they simply slid down and couldn't help themselves. Many people were taken out of the front and, to tell the truth, the promoters were lucky that only two died. Behind the stage was an embankment where they laid out all these kids along the wall. There were a lot of kids. I walked by them on my way to the stage—"You guys okay? You okay? You okay? You okay?" That was fucked up, seeing all the people that had been squashed.

DAVID ELLEFSON: They sold these two-liter bottles of ale and these fans would drink the ale, piss in the bottle, and throw the bottle at the stage. When they'd throw it, piss would come flying out in a big ten-foot wheel of urine. People were throwing mud, not because they hated us, but as a kind of weird salute, the way they gobbed the punk bands. I was strung out. I used my bass as a Viking shield to try to stave off the mud and the piss wheels. Somehow we got through the show.

DAVE MUSTAINE: Some of the things that were coming up on the stage were pieces of the ground, either chunks of grassy clay or soaking mud. Some were hunks of sod. Ellefson got hit a couple of times. My guitar got splattered, but I'm fairly agile onstage and can move around pretty good if I see stuff coming, but I was covered in mud before long.

CHUCK BEHLER: David Ellefson had been doing a lot of smack and he was in withdrawal. You would have never known it, watching him play that day, but he was in pretty bad shape.

DAVE MUSTAINE: We went up onstage to watch David Lee Roth. Lars was there. There are photos of Lars, Slash, and Axl from Guns N' Roses and me sucking on a Jack Daniels bottle backstage after we played. We were all sitting in a circle waiting for one of the other bands to play. Lars was wearing Slash's hat. It was one of the first times I'd run into him at anything significant we were doing, and here we were with this whole thing unraveling around us. That's also where I met British rock photographer Ross Halfin. He was standing in my way and I went to give him a little pinch on his arm to get him out of the way, but I accidentally pinched him too hard. He pulled his arm back and looked up like, Who the fuck did that? Lars and I were both there, so I'm not even sure he knew it was me. I hope he didn't.

CHUCK BEHLER: We went back to the hotel. Junior was sick, really sick. I didn't see him acting that way or feeling that way at all during the show. They held some meetings, evidently, with our manager, Keith Rawls, and agent, Andy Somers, with the two of them in their hotel room later on that night. I didn't really have much to say about it. They made that decision and that's what happened. I wasn't in the hotel room with them. I found out later that night. It wasn't like we had a band meeting. But, to tell you the truth, I really wasn't aware that David had gotten that bad. I really wasn't.

DAVE MUSTAINE: Ellefson was coming out of his skin because he was going into withdrawal really bad. Whenever I went into withdrawal, I just toughed it out. I shook. I sweated. I puked. I shit. I would use alcohol and pot to power my way through it. And they do have stuff you can get over the counter in England to help you get through it, but he didn't want to have any part of that. He wanted to go back home.

This had happened before, earlier in the year. We went to Japan and one of us ran out of heroin. We were supposed to go to Australia after that, but we canceled and came home. That cost us getting banned in Australia for quite a while.

DAVID ELLEFSON: I was so sick all I could do was crawl back to the bus after our set. Kiss, my favorite band growing up, was taking the stage, but I couldn't even lift my head. I sank back in my bunk on the bus and covered my head. I could barely hear them play as the bus pulled out and we left Donington Park for London to catch our flight home. It had been agreed that Dave and I would go into rehab in Van Nuys at a program called ASAP as soon as we got back. It was pathetic.

It was further agreed upon that because I was the one forced to cancel the rest of the dates by my girlfriend that the excuse would be that I fell in the shower, broke my arm. That was the official reason announced as to why Megadeth would be off the remaining shows. They got Testament to fill in for us. And that was it.

DAVE MUSTAINE: But that wasn't it. David Ellefson initially blamed Charlie for us having to cancel those dates. I'm sure today he would admit it was his disease of addiction that caused those cancelation disasters.

ANDY SOMERS: Junior came to me. I was shocked at how strung out and addicted he was. Did I always know Megadeth drank? Yeah. Did I always know there had been drug use, especially with the original lineup? Yeah. They were supposed to continue in Europe, but we pulled those dates down and came home.

DAVE MUSTAINE: I felt shitty. I understood what Ellefson was going through because obviously I'd been through it myself, the withdrawal and everything, but I didn't want to cancel the dates. That was terrible, but it was bittersweet. We were going home and all I was thinking was, go home, get high, and then go check into rehab to see what that will be like.

THE BAND RETURNED to the United States and this lineup of Megadeth—Dave Mustaine, David Ellefson, Chuck Behler, and Jeff Young—never played together again.

TWO

BACK HOME

DAVID ELLEFSON: It was agreed David and I would go in for a ten-day treatment program at a facility in Van Nuys called ASAP. I lasted three days. I was so strung out, I arranged for one of our friends to bring a guitar and gear and hide bags of heroin inside the distortion pedal. Soon we were getting high while we were in rehab. That was the beginning of my journey into sobriety. Clearly, I wasn't ready. I was looking for the just-don't-take-as-much-drugs pill that I could gulp down and get the fuck out of there. After three days, I went home. A couple of days later, Charlie could see I was not serious about being sober and she left.

DAVE MUSTAINE: We were supposed to go into this rehab facility called ASAP in the Valley. This was the first time either one of us had tried treatment. He lasted three days and left. I stayed a little bit longer. He came back, smuggled heroin into the treatment center in a guitar pedal. I got loaded in treatment and checked out. And it was off to the races again.

DAVID ELLEFSON: Megadeth had first started getting deeper into drugs when Gar Samuelson and Chris Poland were in the band. They were fusion jazz musicians from the Dunkirk/Buffalo, New York, area who moved to Los Angeles, where they had a band called the New Yorkers that played around the scene. They built a modest following, selling out the Troubadour and like that, but narrowly missed the window and never got a record deal. Gar was working at B.C. Rich Guitars. Chris Poland had a wealthy girlfriend. The two of them were well funded for their heroin and cocaine habit, which came with them when they joined the band. Dave and I had already certainly been dancing with the cocaine thing because the white lady was popular at the time in LA.

DAVE MUSTAINE: Gar had told me how some friends of the New Yorkers broke into a pharmacy and stole a bunch of opium suppositories. I used to joke about seeing them passed out with their pants off.

Often when we would go into a new city, Gar would disappear. He would head over to the unsavory side of town to find heroin. Sometimes he would come back late, but he always managed to score. That's how Chuck Behler landed the drum job. We were in Detroit and Gar Samuelson went off to go find drugs. When he didn't come back, Chuck saw his opportunity. He had shown up at the club for the sound check and convinced me he knew the songs from the records well enough to play. He sat in before Gar returned. We needed a drum tech anyway, but we hired Chuck because, after that, I knew that if Gar ever messed up, Chuck could play. And that is exactly what happened.

DAVID ELLEFSON: Our first manager, Jay Jones, was our supplier. That was how he ingratiated himself with us. We called it "heroin and hamburgers from Jay Jones." He fed us and kept us strung out. He brought in Gar Samuelson in 1984 and then Chris Poland. I'll never forget the first time I tried heroin. We were rehearsing at Mars Studio, in Los Angeles, and Gar laid out some lines on the counter—a line of white and a line of brown. I asked what the brown line was. He said it was chiba.

"What's chiba?" I said. "Heroin," he answered. I knew about heroin from my punk rock heroes like Sid Vicious and Stiv Bators, not to mention Jimi Hendrix. I knew about it for sure, but Gar said, "Dude, if you want to be great, you've got to do heroin." Half joking. I snorted it up, all the while knowing it was probably not a good idea, but here I was, in Hollywood.

DAVE MUSTAINE: After Castle Donington, the jig was up. But I didn't want to get sober. I was doing my job. The cocaine part was out of control. No question about that. But the heroin was weird. The two drugs had idiosyncrasies. One, you would take and fall asleep and you wouldn't do any more until you woke up; the other one, you would keep doing nonstop, well past the point where you'd had enough, headed to where you can kill yourself. I would wake up in my bed and Ellefson would come into my room and put a mirror under my nose with a line of blow on it. As soon as I started partying, we would go on two-day runs, stay up all night, stay up the next morning, stay up the next day, until I couldn't stay up anymore and I would go to bed. I never fell asleep; I passed out.

Now I had to face that I had an addiction. I mean, I thought it was cool to smoke pot. I thought it was cool to drink. I thought it was cool to go to a party and maybe do a line or something like that. But now it's like I'm some kind of bad guy. That didn't feel good. I kept thinking I'm like Keith Richards now—a junkie. Is that cool? Did I want to get home from Donington? Yes. Did I want to get home to go into rehab? No. I didn't know what was going to happen at rehab and I was afraid. I wanted to go home and get high.

Most guys that have drug problems, it's because they have problems getting the drugs. Guys that have money and can get drugs whenever they want don't have drug problems. They have a drug usage problem. I didn't care, either, about getting clean or about getting loaded; it was simply, at that point, a way of life. I'd accepted that, for me, being loaded was just something that I did.

DAVID ELLEFSON: I tried heroin and I realized it kind of brought me down, took the edge off the cocaine high, which allowed me to do more cocaine. I thought that was wonderful. I called my childhood friends back home in Minnesota and told them I would bring some back for them the next time I came. And I did exactly that when Dave and I made a brief stopover at my parents' farm in early 1986. We had finished the *Peace Sells* album and were headed to New York to get a new manager and meet with the major labels who had started courting us. That was when the heroin thing first started taking hold.

BACK HOME

In summer 1988, we did seven shows on the Iron Maiden Seventh Son of a Seventh Son tour in the United States. We were introduced briefly to the band at the Met Center up in Bloomington, Minnesota, a place with strong emotional memories for me. That was where I saw Kiss—the first band I ever saw—in February 1977. I caught AC/DC, Def Leppard, Blackfoot, and a lot of groups there growing up in Minnesota. We had played there before with Ronnie Dio and now we were back with Iron Maiden, two bands that had a huge influence on me. They parked us backstage down a hallway, in a corner, the better to keep us away. They had young families with nannies, strollers, all the babies and wives. They knew we were trouble. I think the word was pretty prevalent in the business that we did a lot of drugs, that we ran hard and partied hard.

DAVE MUSTAINE: Chuck lived in an apartment complex in Hollywood across the courtyard from our heroin connection, Jay Reynolds. By then, we were buying in bulk—heroin and cocaine by the ounce, either a sixteenth or an eighth. We even briefly used Jay as our guitar player while Chuck was in the band because we thought why not have the dealer in the band? He belonged to a band called Malice and really looked the part. But when it came time to do his guitar parts, Jay said he would have his guitar teacher show him how to play them. I thought, in that case, why not have his guitar teacher in the band instead? So we went with his guitar teacher, Jeff Young. At this time, Jay was living with me and Ellefson at this place in Silver Lake we called the Ranch. I had to go home and tell Jay we had hired his teacher and he was out. That wasn't easy, but we managed to maintain our friendship because Jay wanted to still be our dealer. Chuck was going downhill with the crack pipe and he just kept going down and down. He started selling off his expensive Sonor bubinga wood drum kit. When we were in Nottingham, England, in March 1988—the night after the unforgettable concert in Antrim in Northern Ireland—when Chuck didn't show for a sound check and our drum tech, Nick Menza, jumped up on the drum kit, we knew that Chuck was a thing of the past and that Nick was going to be the new era.

CHUCK BEHLER: I never missed a gig. The one thing that did happen, every once in a while, was that I would let Nick play the drums while I went out into the hall to listen to the drum sound. A lot of the soundmen were not used to that kind of fast drumming and if you don't mix it right in a big arena, it sounds like a bunch of gibberish. So I would go out in the room and have Nick play, not necessarily with the band, but to do a solo or a double-bass beat or something like that so I could hear how the mix was in the room. That may be where Dave realized how good of a drummer Nick was, but I never missed a gig.

DAVE MUSTAINE: Antrim, North Ireland, was where the song "Holy Wars" came from. At the concert, I went outside to sign some autographs. I walked past a little red-headed kid standing by a giant twenty-foot fence. "Fuck you, Dave Mustaine," he said and spit on me. I was furious, but when I got backstage, I learned that the spitting—they called it gobbing—was a sign of respect from punk rockers. Respect? Is that right? Back inside, I heard over the walkie-talkie that somebody was inside the venue selling boot-leg Megadeth T-shirts. I told security to find him, confiscate his shirts, and escort him out. When they found him, he told them he was selling the shirts for The Cause. I had no idea what that meant, but it sounded cool.

I was downstairs talking with one of the locals, still pissed off about being spit on, and getting myself a Guinness when he told me if I drew a happy face in the beer foam, I will always have a drinking partner. I thought that was cute, so I drew a face in the foam and started sipping my Guinness. It occurred to me to ask this nice Northern Irishman "What's 'The Cause'?"

He told me that Ireland was split between the Catholics and the Protestants and they don't like each other. He didn't really go into detail. That was in the back of my mind when I went up onstage to play. It was our first time there and everybody was going mad. There was one kid behind the barricades throwing coins at me. The coins were heavy, like three quarters taped together. You get hit by one, they leave a mark. This guy was throwing these things. I took off my guitar and called him out and the show stopped. I went behind the amps to wait for the green light to go out and play again and there was a regular Sodom and Gomorrah behind the amp line where the stage crew was slamming peppermint schnapps and snorting lines. These guys were having more fun than I was, even though I had already seen a couple of drinking partners smile all the way down. I had a shot of schnapps and some of everything else and went back out. Full of everything and looking out at the crowd, a song I had heard by Paul McCartney popped into my mind, and I thought, "If it's good enough for Sir Paul, it's good enough for me." I walked up to the microphone and said, "Give Ireland back to the Irish. This one is for The Cause."

We slammed into the Sex Pistols song "Anarchy in the UK," which we altered to "Anarchy in Antrim" for the occasion. It was like I had set off a bomb in the audience. It divided the crowd right down the middle, Protestants and Catholics. We were escorted out of town that night in a bulletproof bus, although I still didn't realize the enormity of my gaffe. The next morning, it started to dawn on me when David Ellefson wouldn't speak to me. We left Dublin for Nottingham, which is where Nick Menza sound-checked for Chuck Behler. With everything fresh in my mind, I started writing the lyrics that would become "Holy Wars": *Brother will kill brother spilling blood across the land, killing for religion, something I don't understand.*

DAVID ELLEFSON: We were ready to take the next step for management. Our publicist at Capitol Records, who had previously worked at Elektra, knew Doug Thaler, manager of Mötley Crüe. Thaler was partners with Doc McGhee of the powerful firm McGhee Entertainment. We took a meeting with Doug and he flew out to see us on the So Far, So Good . . . So What! tour. After the Donington show, we made the transition to McGhee Entertainment. One of the main things McGhee had said to me and Dave at their Sunset Boulevard office was that they expected their bands to work hard and be productive because we're here to make a lot of money. We don't care what you do, how you roll, but if you're fucked up on drugs, then you can't be productive. We'll help you get help, but if you can't get help and get clean, then we don't want to have anything to do with you. We're not going to drag incapacitated rock stars around the world. They got

Mötley cleaned up, and some of the Bon Jovi guys, and they were done with that.

CHUCK BEHLER: I didn't go to rehab, but I was using still a little bit on and off, but in support of them I tried not to do it around them when they came back. That probably lasted a couple of weeks. It's not an easy thing. It's not easy. Like Dave says, you have to want to want to stop and only then is when you're going to do it. Other than that, you can fool yourself all you want.

DAVE MUSTAINE: We weren't ready. We were staying up all night doing drugs. Next morning, you know what would happen. Ellefson would walk in and say, "Hey, wake up. Here I am. Here's the mirror. Let's go." My life had gotten out of control. Getting high was everything to me. Music was second and my fiancée Diana was second. At some point, it had just become everything and nothing at the same time.

DAVID ELLEFSON: Dave and I started writing songs to demo in November 1988. Our manager Doug Thaler would come over to my apartment on Cherokee and he would listen to the songs we were writing. Doug would always make the comment that he thought we would write a song and get it to right where it's perfect, and then push the envelope a little too far and add too many parts, too much intricacy. Based on what was on MTV at that time—Mötley Crüe, Twisted Sister, Winger, Dangerous Toys, Nelson—he was probably right.

DAVID ELLEFSON: Right about this time, it was arranged to get some money from Capitol Records—Jeff Young had been let go, but Chuck Behler was still our drummer—to open up a budget to start working on what would become the next album, which, of course, would be *Rust in Peace*.

- THREE -

DEMO

DAVE MUSTAINE: David Ellefson's recollection of details is much more reliable that just about everyone else's. Dates, times, places, etcetera; David must have journaled everything.

CHUCK BEHLER: We finally started rehearsing for *Rust in Peace*. We did a four-track demo on a few songs and went into the Music Grinder—where they did *Peace Sells*—to do a more proper demo of four songs. "Holy Wars" was one and some of the others had different names—the "Rust in Peace" song and two more. It was just the three of us for three days. Casey McMackin, who had worked with us before, engineered the sessions with Dave. There was a pretty good rapport between us, I thought. When we finally did get to working on it, I thought the music was fantastic. I was looking forward to being able to show a lot more of my drumming ability than on the previous record. On that record, I came in so quick, I basically learned it on a couch and had about three weeks to rehearse. I didn't have much time to do anything fancy, although Dave didn't want a lot of extravagant time fills or decorations. He wanted it more straightforward, pounding, thrash-heavy-heavy, so I did my best to accommodate him. At a couple rehearsals, it was just me and Dave going over parts of "Holy Wars," like the end section, and Dave had an amazing command of his guitar parts. He could be high as hell, but when it came to playing the guitar, there was never any problem.

DAVID ELLEFSON: We rehearsed at this tiny, dingy room near Dodger Stadium in Echo Park called Hully Gully. I had been doing so much coke that I started to get sores. We wrote three songs and did a demo of them at a studio in North Hollywood called Amigo Studios, which, by that time, was kind of a dilapidated, rundown studio but had been made famous by producer Michael Wagener on all the records that he had been working on through most of the eighties. He had mixed the *So Far, So Good . . . So What!* record, but he had also mixed *Master of Puppets* for Metallica. He did Dokken records, Accept; he had a pretty shining A-list résumé of really great, popular MTV metal records.

We cut these three tracks and there was a young engineer there named GGGGarth Richardson, and he literally called himself that in his credits. They called him GGGGarth, of course, because he stuttered when he talked. He would go on to have a successful producing career during the late nineties and aughts, but at this point, he was just an engineer. He helped with the writing. The three songs we did were "Holy Wars," which was pretty much written and done in its entirety; "Polaris," which again was written and pretty much done, but it was not called "Rust in Peace . . . Polaris" yet. Another song had the working title of "Child Saints" that Dave put some lyrics on with a melody that never made it to the final. The music of that song was done and it would eventually become "Tornado of Souls," although Dave wouldn't title it "Tornado of Souls" until we were recording the *Rust in Peace* album.

We used the engineer from the *Peace Sells* album named Casey McMackin to add some final overdubs and mix those three songs on the demo at another studio called Track Records. We loved Casey. We felt like Casey understood Megadeth. He was a real rocker. Oddly enough, the manager at the studio was a friend of mine named Alan Morphew, who was a bass player and singer in a band I belonged to briefly in Iowa called Renegade. Al was one of a number of friends of mine who followed me when I moved to Hollywood in 1983.

CHUCK BEHLER: When we were starting to work on the *Rust in Peace* record, there was a lot of drug use going on. I think Dave got into his addiction even more and was using a lot of cocaine, which would make him paranoid. He would think people were against him.

DAVID ELLEFSON: Around this time, I became friends with Slash. He had just come home from the Appetite for Destruction tour and had a run-down little apartment behind Tower Records off Sunset Boulevard. He was like Dave and me. He liked to snort some heroin, snort some coke, and play guitar. We became fast friends. We had good times hanging out, the three of us, but especially Slash and I. We became good guitar-playing buddies.

DAVE MUSTAINE: David had moved from the Ranch to the place on Cherokee with his girlfriend. That's the place where he and I and Slash hung out. We became good friends and even asked Slash to join the band. He thought that was funny; their record was exploding like a rocket, but he actually considered it.

DAVID ELLEFSON: One night, Dave and I sort of tendered the idea to Slash: "Hey, what do you think about maybe joining Megadeth?" We were becoming fast friends and having a lot of fun playing guitar and writing. I think he needed a little time away from Guns N' Roses and it was more a buddy hang, but we did put the idea out there and raised the question. Nothing serious ever came of it.

DAVE MUSTAINE: We needed a guitar player. I called Dimebag Darrell Abbott from Pantera. We knew each other from touring together. The guy had one of my lyrics tattooed on his leg. He made a practice of getting a tattoo from every tour of something that would recall the tour to him. When they went on tour with us, he tattooed a lyric from my song "Sweating Bullets" on his shin. The song talks about a line from one of the spiritual books I read and says something about a black-toothed grin. *Someday you too will know my pain and smile its blacktooth grin.* He liked that blacktooth grin line, and they invented a cocktail they called the black-toothed grin, which, instead of a glass of Coke with a shot of whiskey, was a glass of whiskey with a shot of Coke. Those guys were hard drinkers. And he was this great, shredding guitar player. He liked the idea of joining our band; he said he wanted to do it. I thought this would be the greatest thing ever, but then he asked if he could bring his brother. He founded Pantera with his brother Vinnie Paul Abbott on drums. We already had a drummer. That was a deal-breaker for Dimebag. He wouldn't come without his brother. To this day, I still wonder in wondrous wonder what it would have been like with Vinnie and Darrell.

DAVID ELLEFSON: We had reached out to Diamond Darrell from Pantera, who later was known as Dimebag Darrell but at the time was Diamond Darrell. I had met him one night in Dallas in summer 1988 and we had a bunch of drinks. The next night, I went to see them play at his club in Dallas and they were fucking amazing. They were great, super-tight. They invited me to jump up and play "Peace Sells" with them, which I did. Those boys could drink hard and play their asses off. And Darrell was definitely a guitar star. He was a big deal in the guitar magazines, and Pantera was modestly popular on a more regional level. I talked to Dave about Darrell and we called him up. He basically said his brother Vinnie comes with him or nothing doing. We already had Nick, so we declined and moved on. Also under consideration to be our other guitar player was Jeff Waters of Annihilator. I don't know that we ever reached him, but his band Annihilator was taking off, getting popular, so he essentially proved unavailable, whether or not we ever really connected with him to make the offer. We'd expressed interest and he declined.

DAVE MUSTAINE: I don't know whether Jeff Waters declined or accepted from David Ellefson, because I can't remember us ever making an official call to Jeff. He is a great guitarist, but I think Annihilator is his calling.

CHUCK BEHLER: We had Doug Thaler and Doc McGhee as our management and we would get rehearsal schedules on gold-leaf paper in the mail. It felt really professional, top-notch stuff. But when we were supposed to be at a rehearsal, nobody would show up. I'd go and wait for hours. Sometimes Junior would come. It began to become rare that we all got together. That was not a good sign.

DAVID ELLEFSON: Dave and I started to do a lot of crack. Crack was everywhere, especially in that neighborhood where I lived on Cherokee. We were doing a lot of heroin every day. And I simply melted down. I couldn't take it anymore. I was dating the woman who would become my wife, Julie Foley, who worked for Doug Thaler at McGhee Entertainment, which, of course, was kind of weird because I'm dating the office girl and she's dating the client, which is somewhat taboo, but we hit it off. Julie would stop over to the apartment on Cherokee and me and Dave would be smoking crack and doing heroin and I would always have to hide it from her. Things were getting very weird.

DAVE MUSTAINE: I didn't like Ellefson's girlfriend, Julie Foley. She came over to our apartment, saw that we were getting high, and ratted me out to Doug Thaler, told him that I was doing heroin. Of course, Ellefson had been doing it, too. Everybody had been doing it. But after she shot off her mouth to management, they wanted me to go to a treatment center called Scripps La Jolla in San Diego.

CHUCK BEHLER: Management hooked us up with this guy Bob Timmons, rehab specialist to the stars. He had helped get Mötley Crüe sober. I agreed to go along for the ride to show Dave support. We were going to drive down to San Diego to Scripps. The limo was supposed to pick up Timmons first, but somehow picked up Dave first instead. He showed up at my house about three hours late, just Dave and the limo, and a pile of dope. He said we weren't picking up Bob until it was gone. We drove around Hollywood for another hour and a half getting whacked out of our brains. Finally, I begged Dave, we've got to pick this guy up or Capitol's going to drop us. So, we went and got the Timmons guy. As soon as he got in the limo, he knew what was going on, but he kept his cool and we started going toward San Diego. About fifteen minutes before we arrived, Dave said he was hungry and wanted to stop at a Jack-in-the-Box. You would think this guy, being a drug counselor, would know all the tricks, right? I wasn't hungry, so I stayed in the car while they got out and went to get some food. Dave went in the bathroom at the Jack-in-the-Box for about a half an hour. He came out and, instead of being all talkative from the cocaine, he had evidently done a pile of the other. Back in the limo, Dave started nodding out into his hamburger and Bob's like, uh-huh. He asked Dave if he had anything left he wanted to hand over before we get to this place. Dave looked surprised, like, "What are you talking about?" And nods out. Timmons asked why was he tired all of a sudden. "It must be the Jumbo Jack sauce," Dave said.

DAVE MUSTAINE: I was willing to try this. They had this creepy dude named Bob Timmons, who had been part of a gang in prison. Management enlisted Bob to take me down there, because Aerosmith's manager Tim Collins was our manager Ron Laffitte's hero, so to speak. I soon found out that Bob was not one of the gangbangers so much as one of the girls. Timmons was acting like a hardass with me because I had a joint I wanted to smoke on the way and had left it at my house. I wanted to turn around and get it. Timmons told me no. Immediately, I got pissed and didn't want to go. The remainder of the drive from Hollywood to La Jolla was me fuming and this guy trying to act all tough, clever, and spout platitudes and pontificate about sobriety. I didn't care because all I wanted was to smoke one joint, say goodbye, and then go get sober. I don't know if it was smart or if people do that, but I was basically mourning my friend, the disease, and I was going to say goodbye and try to get sober. That didn't work. I went down to the treatment center and I was there for about a week before I couldn't take it anymore and went home.

DAVID ELLEFSON: We contacted the interventionist Bob Timmons and he helped me get into Brotman Hospital in Los Angeles early February 1989. Dave went into Scripps Hospital in San Diego. Doc McGhee was quite clear: if those guys leave rehab, he said, we're dropping them. Now it was time to get serious. About two weeks into it, Dave left. When I got word that Dave left, I split, too. I was actually starting to feel pretty good in rehab. I had mostly detoxed. I had started going to the gym a little bit. I was attending some twelve-step meetings at Brotman and the lights were coming on. For the first time, I started to think I might separate myself from these drugs. But as soon as I heard my running buddy was out, I was out too. It's amazing how the addict mind-set immediately goes, "Fuck it—I'm out." All my good intentions immediately vanished.

They told me a couple of things in rehab that stuck in my mind. First, they told me there was only one thing I needed to change, and that was everything. That scared me. The other one they said was that they can't take away your talent from you; just stay here, get sober, go through the process, and your talent will always be waiting for you when you get clean.

At this time, there were tons of rock stars getting sober—the Aerosmith guys, Mötley Crüe, David Crosby, Doug Fieger of the Knack. The LA sober scene was now the trendy set; rock stars going to meetings was the new hang. In fact, suddenly drugs and alcohol were no longer cool and the industry was not going to be putting their money on fucked-up, drugged-out rock stars anymore. That was clear.

In rehab, I sat there thinking, "God, if I can just get out there, everything will be fine. My life is out there." But as soon as I was outside the walls of Brotman, I knew it was the wrong move. I shouldn't have left.

During the two weeks while I was there, dope sick, coming off the heroin, I was sitting in a meeting at the big auditorium, completely fucked, and I prayed. I asked God to help me not feel so shitty. Ten minutes later, I was sitting there paying attention to the speaker and I realized my bones had stopped hurting. I'm paying attention to the speaker. I'm not sitting there wallowing in self-pity. I prayed and the result hit me. That made me take notice.

A while after that, I left rehab and another thing they told me started rattling around in my head. They said, if you leave rehab, go back out and get loaded again, you will start off where you left off. It's not like you're getting a reset to when you were fifteen years old, where you could have a couple beers and feel all happy. You're going to pick up right where you left off.

I went straight to see Jay Reynolds. He was passed-out asleep and I knocked on his door until he answered. He wanted to know why I wasn't in rehab. He told me to get out of there, that I was supposed to be sober. But I begged and begged and he finally opened the door and let me in. I did some heroin. I did some coke. And within a few hours, I was more strung out than I'd ever been, just like they said in rehab.

That night in my apartment on Cherokee, I was back in it—the whole rat race of getting loaded, wondering how I am going to get some money when I'm flat broke, and, fuck, I'm going to be jonesing tomorrow.

Fortunately, the next day a friend came by my apartment and sat down in front of me. He told me I was living the dream millions wanted and I was pissing it all away. He said I was being disrespectful to everyone who ever tried because I had it in the palm of my hand and I was throwing it away. He also said that getting help is a sign of strength, not weakness. "So get in my car," he said. "We're going back to rehab. Let's go."

Somehow he got through to me. I got in his car and he took me back to Brotman Hospital. I went back into rehab and this time I stayed for another month-long stint. Meanwhile, during the twenty-four hours I was out of rehab, McGhee Entertainment kept their promise and dropped us from their roster. Now we didn't have a manager, we didn't have a guitar player, and we were fucked.

- FOUR -

DRUMMERS

DAVE MUSTAINE: When it came time to do *Rust in Peace,* we were still putting ourselves through the wringer—drinking, smoking cigarettes, putting heroin in the end of cigarettes. At the end of the night, when we ran out of drugs, we would save just enough to put in one last cigarette. The combination of the nicotine with the heroin and the crack could make you faint. Instead of going to sleep and waking up, you would pass out and come to the next morning. The only thing that would take me off a cocaine high would be putting it in a cigarette with some heroin, and then I was out. Often, we would drive around town in Junior's van, high as could be, and a lyric would come here, a riff would come there.

DAVID ELLEFSON: I went back into rehab. I stayed for almost the entire twenty-eight-day program. This time I ended up getting strung out while I was in there and learned how to smoke heroin. This Iranian guy was having his friends smuggle Persian heroin in to him. He taught me how to smoke heroin off the Winston cigarette tops; the Winston cigarette packs were the only ones with legitimate aluminum foil. So I got strung out again while I was in rehab. The day of my graduation after twenty-eight days, I said fuck it—I'm not even sober. I bailed. That began a round of methadone clinics with Dave. Then I got strung out on methadone, so I was taking heroin, cocaine, and methadone. I would go to the methadone clinic in the morning and a couple hours later, I'd be nodding out and need some cocaine. Then, I would be so tweaked on cocaine, I needed some heroin to come down. By then, I was strung out on all three.

DAVE MUSTAINE: Ellefson met this Arab cat in Brotman who was smoking heroin. He had these Winston cigarettes and he could peel the tin foil off and smoke heroin with it. That's how those guys got high in treatment.

DAVID ELLEFSON: When I got out of Brotman, my friend Richard let me live at his place in Santa Monica, and sometimes Dave would crash there, too. Richard was legitimately sober. He was holding AA meetings in his house and, of course, I was still getting loaded and sneaking out to get high. Dave and I were completely broke. We couldn't afford a pack of cigarettes, gas for the car, or anything. At the last possible minute, a check for $5,000 worth of Metallica publishing showed up for Dave and we lived off that for ages.

We were still staying at Cherokee when Citibank saw fit to send me an American Airlines credit card with a $5,000 cash advance. I went to the ATM, got two hundred bucks out, drove straight to

Jay Reynolds's house, and immediately scored some smack. I was still siphoning off the dregs of that credit card at Richard's when he mentioned one day that his friend Tony Meilandt managed the Fine Young Cannibals whose "She Drives Me Crazy" was, like, number one on MTV at the moment.

DAVE MUSTAINE: Metallica is making millions and I get $5,000 every six months or so. Even still, we still took care of each other.

DAVID ELLEFSON: In spring 1989, we let go of the places on Edgecliffe Terrace and Cherokee and Dave and I moved into a two-bedroom apartment at a little complex called the Studio Colony on Vineland Avenue in Studio City. We did a lot of drugs there.

CHUCK BEHLER: Dave was getting worse. We all were getting worse, but especially Dave. He started missing meetings. We were supposed to meet with someone from the record company at a restaurant one night and nobody could find Dave. I found him. I don't remember how we got to the restaurant. He was really out of it. He was flipping his ashes in his salad and ordering drinks. Days would go by without me talking to anyone and then I would get a call saying a rehearsal was scheduled at this time, and then nobody would show.

DAVID ELLEFSON: At the Studio Colony, Dave and I would be so fucked up, we would stay up all night partying, sleep all day, and miss rehearsal. We would wake up around five or six in the afternoon. We would often snort a line of blow in order to get out the door to rehearsal.

DAVE MUSTAINE: I don't know that I was an alcoholic so much as I was addicted to coke and heroin because if I didn't do coke, I wouldn't drink. If I drank, I would do coke, and then I would drink more. And then, as soon as I did coke, I would need to do heroin because I would get so uncomfortable. I loved the taste of cocaine, but I hated what it made me feel like.

DAVID ELLEFSON: Around this time, Ron Laffitte started circling around. He had been a tour manager for Armored Saint. He had long red hair and looked like a nice, happy version of Bruce Dickinson. It was his intention to manage Megadeth and he knew his way to Dave was through me. In summer 1989, he was buying me dinner at a Mexican restaurant on Melrose Avenue, wanting to get in the loop with Megadeth.

We had met Ron before, when he was working for Rod Smallwood. During the *So Far, So Good . . . So What!* period, we took a meeting with Ron over at Rod Smallwood's office on Highland Avenue in Hollywood. At the time, Rod was at the top. Iron Maiden was huge. He had just signed Poison and brought them to Capitol Records. He had signed W.A.S.P. He had a great roster and was pretty much ambassador to all things heavy metal and hard rock to Capitol Records and EMI. Rod didn't really get Megadeth or he wasn't that interested. I think he saw us as a little too rough, unrefined, and so that meeting with Ron didn't work out.

A year later, Ron was back, sniffing around. I told Dave I thought we should take a meeting with this Ron Laffitte. We didn't have a manager. Tony Meilandt came and went. McGhee Entertainment was long gone. Ron had the right temperament. He was a nice guy, caring, a hard worker. His agenda was to be in management. He studied the business. He had made connections over at EMI and Capitol and EMI Music Publishing. It became his life aim to manage Megadeth. And we decided to let him.

One afternoon, I came back to Studio Colony after scoring some drugs and Ron was hanging out with Dave in the kitchen. I broke down and cried. Ron looked me in the eye, and he was kind of tearing up too. He talked straight to me. "If you really want help," he said, "I'll do everything I can and I'll drop everything to help you." And I said, "You know what? I do. I want help."

He introduced us to a Hispanic drug and alcohol counselor named John Bocanegra. Dave and I started seeing John in private sessions. I was meeting with him twice a week. We started to do band meetings with him. Ron was getting advice from Tim Collins, the Aerosmith manager who dragged those guys through rehab into sobriety.

DAVE MUSTAINE: I was being taken care of by a Dr. Marks, who, ironically, we met through one of our drug connections. He was having some success working with some of the Guns N' Roses guys using an experimental drug called Buprenex. The drug would fend off the effects of opiate withdrawal, an injection that worked instantly, although it made it hard for me to stay awake. He was also giving me another drug that came in a tablet.

DAVID ELLEFSON: A doctor we knew in Hollywood named Dr. Marks had a medication called Buprenex by a company called Burroughs Wellcome, probably the equivalent of today's Suboxone. You would draw it up in a tiny diabetic needle out of the jar and give yourself a skin prick in the fat of your belly or butt. Dave and I were both doing this stuff. He was trying to help rock stars get cleaned up with this stuff without having to go into big, long, expensive residential rehabs.

DAVE MUSTAINE: Chuck was falling apart. Junior saw him coming out from under a house in the neighborhood where he had been smoking crack.

DAVID ELLEFSON: Chuck Behler was down at the bottom as well. He was living in an apartment in Hollywood with his girlfriend and their baby. He was completely unavailable to the band, strung out and broke. He was trying to be a dad and had no money.

CHUCK BEHLER: The girl I was with, we were starting to get really serious and she got pregnant. I don't know if that scared Dave, if he didn't want a guy in his band with a kid. I was spending a lot of time with her. Because of the drugs, of course, me and the girl were having problems. I was trying to quit, but that was really hard.

I didn't go to rehab at that time. I just tried to do it myself. We started arguing and she went home to her mom in Connecticut right after the baby was born and that crushed me.

DAVE MUSTAINE: Chuck crawled into a crack pipe. He was selling his drum kit and whenever we wanted to go rehearse, we had to track him down and find his gear.

CHUCK BEHLER: Dave came over. I hadn't seen him in a month or so, and I know he noticed that I wasn't doing too well. My girlfriend had moved out. I was all by myself in the apartment. Dave had a bunch of stuff on him and I thought he came over to talk with me since I wasn't doing that good, but he just wanted to get high. He wanted something—I can't remember what—but I couldn't help him and he split. After that, I didn't see anyone. No calls, no nothing.

DAVID ELLEFSON: Dave had asked me to go over and audition Nick Menza. I went over to this small studio at the west end of the Burbank Airport runway. He had been hanging in the wings for the last year and a half as a kind of understudy to Chuck Behler. Nick basically served as the drum tech, drove the truck, and was like a roadie for us through the *So Far, So Good . . . So What!* campaign.

Nick smoked pot and drank, but did not do hard drugs. He was a stoner Valley boy who could be a little wild and was wired more like a lead singer. He always wanted to be in the spotlight. He fancied himself a guitar player/songwriter/singer/painter/artist kind of guy. But he had great energy on the drums and was athletic. His dad was Don Menza, a highly esteemed jazz saxophonist/woodwind player and arranger. He arranged and played first chair tenor sax for Buddy Rich and Louie Bellson. It's almost like Nick rebelled against his jazz musician father by being a rock and roller.

Nick and I went in and rehearsed. He was a bit of a runaway train with the tempos. He would start at one tempo, get going, and I would have to pull him back. I came home from the audition and Dave asked how it was. I told him I thought Nick was the guy. He was all we had and now his time was here.

DAVE MUSTAINE: The voices in my head were nonstop chatter. They told me, "This is the one thing that you had that gave you any kind of self-worth, and now look at you; you could have been so much better and you're not." The voices kept getting louder and louder—"You suck. You really do suck. You *should* have been kicked out of Metallica. You *should* have been kicked out of Megadeth too." A lot of the little stuff, the fighting, the accusations, it was galvanizing me. I was hardened to where, anytime anyone said something to me, my knee-jerk reaction would be "I don't care."

I did care, but it was getting to a point where there was so much whining, complaining, and money problems that by the time we parted ways with Chuck, it was a relief. Nick was fun, upbeat. He wasn't doing coke and heroin. He liked to smoke pot; that was it. He had a beautiful, loving mom, and his dad played with Henry Mancini on "Pink Panther." Nick was a life-of-the-party-type guy, but he did have ambitions. Every chance he got, he would come up to me and David and whisper in our ears Chuck was a "fat fucking pig" and that he belonged up there.

CHUCK BEHLER: Nick was like competition from day one. I wasn't supposed to know, but I figured the deal out right away. He didn't sabotage me or anything, but he sure as hell didn't go out of his way to make things easier for me. He did what he was supposed to do, kept the drums tuned and set up every night, but in his mind, from the very beginning, he was thinking he was going to get this gig.

I got a mailbox full of tax statements and stuff like that from the financial guys, who also wrote that they were not going to pay my rent anymore. Basically, that was it. Nobody said I was fired. I was broke and couldn't do anything but go back to Detroit. Shortly before I left, Gar and another friend dropped by and told me Nick was playing drums. That was how I found out. I never even called and asked. I went home and that was it.

DAVE MUSTAINE: Funny how Chuck is still in denial that his kit wasn't being tampered with each night. Nick was adjusting his drum pedals every show to make it easier or more difficult to play. Each pedal has two springs for tension on each side, and Nick was responsible for setting those pedal tensions for the drummer each night. Yeah, Chuck figured it out right.

FIVE

GETTING STRAIGHT

TONY LETTIERI: My friend Ron Laffitte called and said he had a band that needed some help. The guys weren't producing. They were in kind of a bad way and needed somebody to be with them and help them through some stuff, maybe do some tech work. I wasn't familiar with Megadeth at the time, but Ron set up a meeting with Dave, Junior, and Nick Menza at a sushi restaurant on Ventura Boulevard. I had studied martial arts and been a boxer when I was young, so I did some bodyguard-type work, which was also something they were looking for. Everything kind of meshed.

Dave and Junior were living in a two-bedroom apartment in North Hollywood and they were in terrible shape. The next day I went to pick up Dave, and the apartment was a complete mess. They would sit around the coffee table, which was covered with all sorts of paraphernalia, in this dark apartment—not a productive situation. My instructions were to get Dave healthy, get the band back in the studio, get them right again, and simply to be there.

DAVE MUSTAINE: We had some minders. I had a guy named Tony Lettieri, who went on to become a detective, a DEA agent, and a law enforcement officer in Nevada. He was my bodyguard. He was the one who helped me train and ultimately introduced me to Sensei Benny "The Jet" Urquidez, a world-class Hall of Fame martial artist with nine black belts.

TONY LETTIERI: Dave was very difficult. In the beginning, it was a nightmare. He was not in a great mood. He was always wanting to use and do his own thing. But we were under directive from the record company that if they didn't get something going soon, it was going to be bad news for the band. I stayed with him on a daily basis and took him to appointments. We started having band meetings at my house in Sherman Oaks.

Dave was seeing a doctor who was treating him with an experimental medicine. I carried this medicine because it needed to be administered to Dave every so many hours to keep him cool. Dave and I spent all our days and nights together for quite a while and did just about everything together. He was getting geared up to get going with his career again, writing songs for *Rust in Peace,* and going back into rehearsals.

RANDALL KERTZ: I knew Ron Laffitte from when he was road manager for Armored Saint and I ran a record store in Chicago. After I moved to Los Angeles in February 1989 to study bass at the Musicians Institute, we ran into each other and he offered me a job with Megadeth, which I didn't take right away. I met Ron and Nick Menza for lunch; they laid out the situation and I said okay.

I was assigned to David Ellefson, who was living in Studio City. Both Daves were going through rehab programs. Nick Menza had just come on board as the drummer. They didn't have a guitar player at the time. I didn't see Dave Mustaine for the first couple of months.

I was a green twenty-two-year-old, just making it up as I went along. I think they hired me because I was new out there, a good kid from the Midwest, and wasn't really yet corrupted. I wasn't on drugs of any kind, which they probably thought would be helpful.

Junior went with the program. He understood the importance of the program and he followed it. When I first showed up, they were on the Buprenex, the shots, the whole works. The Buprenex was the next best thing after methadone, and the hope was that after they were weaned off Buprenex, there would be no more anything. As it went on, Ellefson became less dependent on the Buprenex, more active, and less dependent on me. He started to lose some weight and get back in shape. The next step was for me to start setting up the gear in the rehearsal studio so he and Nick could get together during the day, make music, hash out some ideas, waiting for the return of Mustaine.

I didn't meet Mustaine until a couple months after I started. I went to Junior's house one morning with the coffee and donuts and Mustaine answered the door. We had not met before. He had left rehab, went over to Junior's, and they scored. Then it was time to get back with Dr. Marks. He told me to make some calls and I did. That was the first meeting with Mustaine.

DAVE MUSTAINE: I was living with Tony Lettieri, trying to get straight, when we went into the studio to record the old Alice Cooper song

"No More Mr. Nice Guy" for the Wes Craven film *Shocker*. We were working with Desmond Child as producer. He was a top songwriter who wrote all those hits for Bon Jovi, Aerosmith, Cher, and others. He was pop and I was heavy metal.

We didn't get along well at all, and I spent a lot of time on the opposite side of my amp, where I didn't have to see him. I adjourned frequently to the roof of the studio because I was having such a horrible time. He wanted me to do all these poppy, quadruple-tracked choruses and background vocals and play these syrupy chords. I thought, "I can't, I can't, I can't, I can't, I can't."

DAVID ELLEFSON: We went in the Record Plant with producer Desmond Child. He was as successful as you get in the record business. We listened one afternoon intently, up on the roof, Dave and me, smoking crack, as Desmond gave us the talk—if you guys can just get it together, you guys could be huge. That talk.

DAVE MUSTAINE: Ron Laffitte was insistent that I do all this. I complained that we weren't even our usual four-piece, only a trio. He said the guitar tech, Sport, could play acoustic on the track. I freaked when he said that, but I eventually went along.

DAVID ELLEFSON: To direct the video, we went with Penelope Spheeris, who we knew. She had directed *The Decline of Western Civilization*, which included the "In My Darkest Hour" video from *So Far, So Good . . . So What!*, which she also directed. She used our version of "These Boots Are Made for Walking" in a film she directed called *Dudes,* starring Jon Cryer, Lee Ving, and Flea from Chili Peppers. We had a history with Penelope. But the video turned out to be a disappointment to me because everybody was pandering to Dave. It was quickly clear that Dave was going to be the star of this video, and Nick Menza and I were relegated to what was essentially a cage, a jail cell, singing one chorus of the song and that was it. It was a struggle. We weren't really sober yet, but we were turning that corner, and it wasn't lost on me that if a lot of drug use didn't fuck up our friendship, a little bit of sobriety sure did.

TONY LETTIERI: At the height of this medication he was taking under Dr. Mark's care, Dave was out of it. Sometimes he could barely stand. I took him to the shoot. Ron Laffitte met us there. Penelope could see that he was not in great shape and the shoot was difficult. He was barely capable. She put him on this revolving stage and he was supposed to be playing a guitar solo while the stage spun around, but he had no equilibrium. They had me behind him out of camera range because he kept falling over. They shot him from the waist up while I ducked down holding on to his belt loop while this stage spun. It was a mess.

DAVE MUSTAINE: Ron Laffitte, the same guy who was coaching me through the session with Desmond Child, was telling me, "Dave, you can do this." Penelope had me on this pedestal, like a lazy Susan, except not sturdy, wobbly. It started turning and she told me, "Look at the camera." I turned and looked, turned and looked. I had to turn my head around to follow the camera and then turn it back the other way to start again. I was fucked up on psychopharmaceuticals. I was dizzy. I couldn't do this—spinning around, looking over my shoulder, looking over the other shoulder, trying to play guitar at the same time. My hair was in my face. I was up there by myself. I was lucky to get as much done as I did. I was in a sad state.

When it came time to film the one scene that showed the entire band, I complained that we were not a three-piece band and we were missing a guitar player, so in the scene in the jail cell, there's a fourth guy in the back, just a shadow with long hair, played by Ron Laffitte. I'm sure Penelope probably was a little frustrated. It was an inopportune time for her to see me like that; I was still getting from point A to point B, moving away from being a functioning heroin addict.

DAVID ELLEFSON: Ron Laffitte had just taken a job for a larger management company called Lippman and Kahane run by two brothers, Michael and Terry Lippman, and Rob Kahane. Kahane managed George Michael, who was at the peak of his career. Terry Lippman was a producer/manager, and Michael Lippman kind of reminded me of Michael Caine. We held the premiere for the "No More Mr. Nice Guy" video at the China Club in Hollywood. Alice Cooper came out. His latest record was *Trash,* a huge success, and Desmond Child had written songs with him for that. Alice was, by then, very sober. We were not sober. Especially Dave. The Lippmans were there with Ron Laffitte, and they were not pleased.

There comes a time when you don't know if you want to be sober, but you certainly don't want to be as fucked up as you are and you don't want to be strung out anymore. I don't know that Dave ever really wanted to be sober. But everybody in the business was serious about it: *Dave needs to get clean. We can't work with the guy. He's got to get clean.*

DAVE MUSTAINE: They wanted me to come to the stupid release party and act like I was being electrocuted. I was so not into the idea. I mean, how dumb is that? I was supposed to get into a jumpsuit, get strapped into a chair, and pretend like I was being electrocuted. I went through the whole thing, but I really didn't like it.

RANDALL KERTZ: We were doing this song to keep Megadeth in the game while everybody got it together behind the scenes. We held a video release party for a bunch of industry people at the Palace. Tony and I dressed in hoods and black outfits and carried out Mustaine in an orange jumpsuit, straight off the movie poster. We put him in this chair and he kept getting up. He was supposed to act like he was breaking loose, but I pushed him back a little too hard and the whole damn thing almost fell over. That didn't go over too big. Then somebody else came out in a hood and, when he took it off, it was Alice Cooper. He pulled the switch and electrocuted Mustaine.

DAVE MUSTAINE: I was bouncing back and forth between a slightly seedy old hotel on Hollywood Boulevard and my mother's place in Elsinore. I was dealing with Dr. Marks, the Buprenex injections in my stomach, the pills, the driving from Elsinore to see him, and all of the madness that had started to take over my life from the drugs and alcohol. With Nick firmly in the band, we began to spend more time writing songs for the new album, even as out of control as things were.

David and I would roll around in his van and I would come up with little lyrical tidbits or stuff. We would be wherever we were at the time, which usually wasn't anywhere special. We were hardly ever anywhere and when we were, we were always loitering wherever we went. It was like we were waiting. Waiting for success. Waiting for the drugs to kick in. Waiting for inspiration. Waiting to score. Waiting to stop using the drugs. Waiting for this damn purgatory to end when we would no longer be waiting, but we would finally be there. Wherever "there" was. Until then, we would loiter in Junior's van, driving around. I wrote the lyrics to "Lucretia" in the back seat, feeling so fucking hopeless. *Sitting up, late at night, I tiptoe through the darkness . . .*

A lot of that late-night lyrics writing was fueled by cocaine, although "Hangar 18" was on the other side of all of that partying and stuff because I'd already come out of the treatment center. I was with an artist and repertoire guy from Capitol assigned to me named Josh Deutsch, who was the guitar player from Cyndi Lauper. "Hangar 18" had been kicking around since my days in Panic. He made a suggestion to say something about an alien because he thought the song was about aliens. I came up with the words. I wasn't going to sing about some alien; that's where we ended up with the two words "foreign life":

> *Foreign life forms inventory*
> *Suspended state of cryogenics*
> *Selective amnesia's the story*
> *Believed foretold but who'd suspect*

GETTING STRAIGHT

The military intelligence
Two words combined that can't make sense
Possibly I've seen too much
Hangar 18, I know too much.

RANDALL KERTZ: Even when he was nearly out of it, Mustaine could be wicked funny. Junior and I went with him to this panel discussion Bob Chiappardi's heavy metal marketing company Concrete Marketing was throwing. Mustaine was going to be on the panel. He hadn't been seen in public for a while and he wasn't looking all that good. Plus, he was taking Dr. Marks's drugs and they had a tendency to make him sleepy and mess with his memory. He would nod from time to time.

There were about five or six other musicians with him on the dais. One of them was Don Dokken. Mustaine walked in after everybody else, kind of last minute, and took his seat on the end. A buzz went through the crowd. Not only was he a big star, he hadn't been around much lately. He was pale and barely moving. He looked like he could drop on the spot. He had his head down, his eyes closed, and nobody knew what was happening. At some point, somebody asked Don Dokken about his plans and Don Dokken said he was thinking about pursuing a solo album. All of a sudden, Mustaine snapped his head up and he said, "What are you going to call it, 'Don'?"

DAVE MUSTAINE: I was staying with my mom in Elsinore, away from temptation and connections. Our guitar tech Sport would drive down and bring me the medicine. I figured if I was down there, I didn't know anybody, and I would be forced to go through whatever I had to go through until he would come with the medicine. That was pretty much the end of Dr. Marks.

Elsinore was also where I was introduced to skydiving. The whole thing began when I told some interviewer I *wanted* to go skydiving and she got it wrong and wrote that I *went* skydiving. Now I figured I had to. It was too late to retract. I was on a high-adrenaline diet at the time and although it was scary, it was exactly the rush I was looking for. I was hooked.

I was driving back from Perris Valley Skydiving Center out by Lake Elsinore, California, when I pulled up on the rear end of a funky old car rolling north on Interstate 5. I saw this bumper sticker: MAY ALL YOUR NUCLEAR WEAPONS RUST IN PEACE. I knew instantly what my new album title was going to be.

- SIX -

BACK TO REHAB

TONY LETTIERI: We got Dave into a twelve-step program eventually. I took him to check in to rehab at the Beverly Hills Medical Center. That was where John Bocanegra entered the picture. He was the director of the rehab program.

DAVE MUSTAINE: When John Bocanegra came in, he was helpful. For some crazy reason, I respected him. He had been a bank robber and done all these bad things that made me think he was cool. He looked like Pancho Villa, short Mexican, hair parted down the middle, with a big bandito moustache. When I met him, he had been facing seventeen years in prison. He was working at Beverly Hills Medical Center, but before that he was at a place called Impact Drug and Alcohol Treatment Center in Pasadena that specialized in only the hardest of the hardcore, junkies, gangbangers, parolees. He had been diverted there by court after killing a security guard in a bank robbery. He told me about his drug-running days, and he was a certified badass—but I liked him and thought he was cool. He got sober at Impact and discovered that he had a gift for helping other people leave drugs behind. He knew how to talk to people. He knew how to talk to me. But I would soon find out the guy I thought was a miracle healer was more like Typhoid Mary.

DAVID ELLEFSON: I was meeting every week with John Bocanegra, the counselor. I was making the attempt. I wasn't there yet. I was not quite over the hump. And Dave was feeling somewhat resentful about having to be sober, too. He mandated that everybody around him had to be clean: if I've got to be clean, fuck you, you're all going to be clean too. This went so far as Nick Menza showing up at rehearsal wearing a Corona beer T-shirt. Dave would lambast him. "You can't wear that shirt—you could make me relapse—take it off." That did not go well with Nick, who didn't think he had any substance abuse issues and could help himself to a beer if he felt like it. They butted heads over this and our manager Ron Laffitte had to take Nick aside and tell him to go along with the program for the greater good. That's the way things went with Dave. You're not going to change his mind; just change the shirt.

He had Rob Kahane, one of the partners in Lippman and Kahane, pull me into his office and tell me, "Dave says you need to be sober or you're out of the band." I was so fucking pissed. I asked, "Why couldn't Dave tell me that?" Kahane said, "He asked me to do it." Get clean or you're out of the band, he told me. Use, you lose. As much as it infuriated me, I knew I needed to get clean. I was trying.

DAVE MUSTAINE: That's the first thing I have ever heard of that.

TONY LETTIERI: The rehab was tough. I'd go to the AA meetings and Al-Anon meetings with Dave, and John would come to my house for band meetings.

DAVE MUSTAINE: We would hold these band meetings where we would all sit in a circle with me in the middle and Bocanegra would run the show. They weren't band meetings so much as psych sessions, although Bocanegra was no licensed therapist. He was simply picking up on techniques he learned at the medical center. As soon as these meetings were done, I would get in my little gray Mercedes and drive straight to a liquor store. Those meetings were hard for me. They would bash me to the point where I was crying on the inside, but I wouldn't let them see me cry on the outside. I would go buy two bottles of vodka. Then I would go score some drugs.

TONY LETTIERI: Dave had people around him that always wanted to give him drugs. I was there to keep these people out, people I was told who weren't good for him to be around. We went out one night to see the Cult play at Long Beach Arena, and this guy backstage kept coming up, trying to hand off a packet to Dave while I was with him. I finally had to take the guy, grab him by the throat, hold him against the wall, and tell him not to do that.

DAVE MUSTAINE: Every time I went to the Beverly Hills Medical Center, I would get detoxed and I would feel better when I would leave. As soon as I left, the same fucking problems I had when I went in there were waiting for me.

DAVID ELLEFSON: We would do weekly group counseling sessions—Ron, Dave, Nick, and me—often at Tony Lettieri's place, but sometimes at my new apartment on Colfax that Randy helped me move into early fall 1989. There was always something a little uncomfortable about that apartment. I always had this weird, eerie feeling like someone was hovering over me, watching me sleep in my bed. It was the strangest thing. One day Nick Menza came over and was hanging around the swimming pool, chatting up some of the girls who lived in the building. He tells them which apartment his friend lived in and they told him the previous tenant was a Vietnam veteran who blew his head off with a shotgun in the apartment. Furthermore, turned out down the hallway was where the Playboy Playmate Dorothy Stratten of the movie *Star 80* was murdered.

RANDALL KERTZ: They wanted Junior to move, so we found this new place for him on Colfax. The vibe was never right, even before we found what had happened in the apartment. One of the first serious conversations I had with Mustaine was when he told me to move Junior again. "I know about witchcraft," he told me. He said he knew about vibrations and I had to get him out of there. "It's dangerous," he said. Mustaine couldn't have been more serious, forthrightly telling me about all the bad juju and how we had to take this seriously or there would be consequences.

DAVID ELLEFSON: I got out of there immediately, broke my lease, tried to get my money back, and didn't care when I couldn't. I moved to a brand-new apartment complex at Vineland and Moorpark. Under my new mandated sobriety program, I was required to meet with John Bocanegra twice a week at his apartment in Venice. John really helped me turn the corner into my sobriety. He started working with me through twelve-step literature. Slowly the lights were coming on.

DAVE MUSTAINE: I didn't want to get sober. I was being forced to get sober. I was living with Tony Lettieri at the time. I had my own place, but Tony was trying to help me get straight. I was super impressed with Tony. He was this slick Italian-Jewish kid with a good build—maybe slightly overweight, but solid. Not only was he a black belt, but he was also a Mensa kid. I did not know many of those and, in fact, didn't even know what Mensa was. I looked up to him, liked, and respected him.

Tony introduced me to this guy named Randy Cervantes, who was highly skilled with many martial arts weapons. Tony thought it would be a good idea for me to meet him and invited Randy over one afternoon. Watching Randy go through some of his moves, his *katas* and the forms, I got excited about picking training back up. It had been a long time. Tony got it. "You need to go see the Jet," he said.

"The Jet?" I said.

"Benny 'The Jet' Urquidez," he said.

If you're in the martial arts game and have any knowledge of the history or the hierarchy, you would know Sensei Benny, although I didn't. Yet. He can be seen fighting with Jackie Chan in the movies, where, of course, he always loses, but he is Chan's respected peer and has been around the scene many long years. I went to start training with him and it completely changed my outlook toward life. I have said that Sensei Benny helped save my life.

But I still had a long way to go. I was still sleeping on Tony's couch and using cigarettes as a vehicle to get drugs out of my system. I was smoking like a fiend. When I finally got my own apartment and moved out, he pulled the couch away from the wall. There were marks all over where I'd been putting out my cigarettes on the wall and I didn't know that. Sorry, Tony.

DAVID ELLEFSON: John could see through my bullshit in a second. When I told him I was going to lay off the heroin and cocaine and stick to smoking pot and drinking, he burst out laughing. "When was the last time you smoked pot and drank and *didn't* end up on heroin and cocaine?" he said.

He fucking nailed me. I would go over to Nick Menza's place in North Hollywood, where he lived with his girlfriend, Stephanie. They had this open-door policy, his friends coming and going all the time, very friendly, very open. People didn't even have to knock; just walk in. I liked that about them. When I grew up on the farm in Minnesota, people dropped over all the time. We left the keys in the car. We never locked the house. Nick had this same kind of community.

Nick would be sitting around smoking weed and ask me, "Hey, dude, you want to take a bong hit?" I'd take a hit. A little while later, I'd get cotton mouth and Nick would offer me a beer. I'd have a couple beers as we watched *The Simpsons* or *Married with Children*. It wouldn't take long for my mind to start thinking I needed to go see my new dealer in Santa Monica. I'd think, "Fuck, I've got to get over to see him and get some coke because I'm starting to get tired." Once I was there, I figured I might as well get some heroin, because I know I'm going to need that. Sure enough, like Bocanegra said, I would end up on pot, booze, coke, and heroin. Those were the four horsemen of my apocalypse of my drug addiction.

I saw John twice a week. Dave, I think, was seeing him three times a week. I had this calendar in my new apartment on Vineland, and I kept having to change the sobriety date. It was November 1 was day one. I marked the calendar. Then it was day two, day three, four. . . . I didn't drink, I didn't cop, I didn't smoke any dope today. I was praying, starting the first night in my apartment, and I was really a mess. I prayed, oh God, please help. Through that prayer and obviously many others after that, I put together a month clean. I was still taking the Buprenex from Dr. Marks, which I understand today would not constitute true sobriety. But after a month, suddenly the obsession returned. I was going to go get a thirty-day chip at a meeting and detoured to my dealer's place in Santa Monica to cop. I didn't tell anyone.

The next day I was full of guilt and felt shitty. I moved the sobriety date on the calendar.

TONY LETTIERI: We were in rehearsals in the Valley. Dave was starting to get back into the music more. He was writing the songs. And no matter what, his guitar playing was always great. They were looking at different guitarists to come on board.

DAVE MUSTAINE: We looked for a long time. There weren't that many guys, but we kept looking. This guy wasn't right for this reason, this one, for that. We had one cattle-call audition where some guy showed up and told me he had written my song "Wake Up Dead." I was stunned—I didn't even know the guy, and he was telling me he wrote one of my songs.

TONY LETTIERI: I met my girlfriend at the same rock club in the Valley where Dave met Pam right around the same time. They knew each other. They were both horse-riding girls from the Valley. The four of us didn't hang out too much, but everybody sort of knew each other out there in the Valley.

DAVE MUSTAINE: It was the singer from Nick Menza's side project, Von Skeletor, who asked me to come out the night I met my wife. He was a member of the Guns N' Roses camp and newly sober. He asked me to go with him to a nightclub in the Valley called FM Station to help keep him sober. He was fresh out of rehab and heard I was clean. He asked me to help him stay clean for the night, so I took one of my buddies and out we went.

That was where I saw Pam. She was so attractive to me that I couldn't even approach her myself. I sent my buddy over to ask her if she would talk with me. She told him if I wanted to talk with her to come over and talk with her myself.

I didn't want to go into the whole explanation about how I was out baby-sitting a fellow heroin addict new to sobriety and such, so I simply walked up and said, "Hello, my name is Dave." She snapped, "I know who you are." I continued and told her I was with friends tonight, but that I would like to take her to lunch tomorrow. It was an unconventional approach, but it spoke of my sincerity.

The next day we had our big date, but again not without some unintended drama. I had become very close with my bodyguard, Tony, and, at the time, I didn't know how to show anybody—let alone someone as important to me as Tony—that I liked them. I did what I always did—I bought stuff. I went and bought Tony a $3,000 Rottweiler puppy, but it took forever to be delivered, which happened to be the same day I was supposed to go out with Pam. I waited and waited, all the while calling Pam and saying I would be right there. Finally, they showed up, gave me the dog. I grabbed it, hauled ass to Tony's house, gave Rommel the Rottweiler to Tony, and raced off to see her.

PAM MUSTAINE: My roommates and I would go to FM Station just to get out of the apartment. It was convenient and right around the corner from where we lived. It really wasn't my scene. I had quit drinking and was drinking water that night. Dave was there with his security guard and some of his other buddies checking out a band to produce. Dave sent his security guard over to let me know that Dave wanted to meet me, and I let him know that if he wanted to meet me, he can come over himself.

I was career-oriented and at the time worked for Arbitron, and before that a talent agency. I wasn't into heavy metal; that whole form of music was not my vein, and I didn't want anything to do with it. It only meant trouble to me. I was getting ready to go when Dave came over and introduced himself. He asked me if he could take me to lunch, and my roommate and I at the time had made a decision we would never turn down an offer for food. We ended up going to lunch. He was late picking me up, because he was delivering a dog for his security guard, which he had bought as a birthday gift for him. All this was not my style.

The lunch was good. It turned to dinner another time, where he told me that he was a couple weeks out of treatment. I had never been around heroin, I didn't even know what that looked like. On our way to dinner, I noticed Dave coming close to hitting the parked cars along Ventura Boulevard. I stuck around and found out later that he had fallen off the wagon. He had, at the time, a drug counselor working with him. He was doing everything to do right by himself, and it all looked like the behavior of somebody wanting to sort his life out and do right, so I admired that. I thought it was honorable that a guy would take the time to switch lanes and respect and honor himself enough to do something about it. To me, that had value.

DAVE MUSTAINE: That night, we went out. When I took her home, I kissed her goodnight on the front step of her apartment. She told me later that she felt my kiss go right through her. She felt like she'd known me all her life. I felt something strange like that too. I knew she was going to be my soul mate.

PAM MUSTAINE: When I kissed him goodbye, it felt like I went through him to the beginning of time. I've never had anything like that happen before. It was the weirdest experience. The thing is, the two of us would never have come together, ever, had we not crossed paths that night by accident at FM Station. Our worlds did not mix. But that's what happened. There was something there, and we got to actually see who each of us really were, and that's who we fell in love with. People choose to see it or not, but it's all about vulnerability and how vulnerable you'll allow someone to be so that they can see the depths of who you are. But we were able to go there with each other, and I knew we were created for each other.

DAVE MUSTAINE: I knew she was the one, but the problem was there was already somebody else. I was going to have to get rid of the other girl. I had moved out of Tony's into some temporary quarters at the Oakwood, a sprawling complex on the hill above Warner Brothers in Burbank, where a lot of musicians find short-term housing. Rick James died there. The other girl had a key to my apartment. Pam did not. Pam and I went to eat Chinese food at Chin Chin's for dinner and got into an argument on the ride home. I was pissed because she confessed that she had an eating disorder. We made it back to my place, and she was lying down on my couch when the front door opened and in burst the other girl. I had not had the opportunity to tell her about Pam and I had certainly not told Pam about her.

The other girl turned on her heels and ran back out the door. In my haste and confusion, I ran after her. I didn't know why I was doing that, running after the girl I didn't want while the one I wanted was back in my apartment. Only she was gone when I got back. Pam had split. I had lost two girls in ten seconds. I called Pam to try and get back with her, but she turned me down.

PAM MUSTAINE: In that day, people saw whoever they wanted, and I had a boyfriend at the time. Nobody knows if you're going to end up with this person, so everybody's doing other things. In LA, you learn survival skills. Dave and I had seen each other a few times. I had been staying over at his place, and I had some of my stuff over there. He had given me a key. I had my own issues paralleling his, and my eating disorders were now full-blown. I was laying on the sofa, not feeling well. A girl he had been seeing showed up at his door, and he opened it a crack to talk with her. He told her she couldn't come in because his friend was not feeling well. He pushed her out in the hall and when he followed to talk with her, I grabbed a trash bag, put my clothes in it, left his key on the counter, and left. I took my phone off the hook, and that was that.

TONY LETTIERI: I took Dave to Hawaii that Christmas. His family didn't celebrate and I had family on the North Shore of Hawaii.

DAVE MUSTAINE: I needed to get away from things and think. I needed to know what this girl was to me. I went to Hawaii with Tony to try and sort out my feelings for her. I was miserable without her. I could see I had genuine feelings for her. We clearly had two different recollections of that night.

PAM MUSTAINE: This little short, fat Latino with a handlebar moustache showed up at my door in North Hollywood. He looked like a killer. My first thought was that somebody was trying to do a drug deal and they got the wrong house. Then he said he was a friend of Dave's, and I went, "Nope, nope, nope, nope—I'm not doing this." "Hear me out," he said. Dave had sent him over. He told me he was Dave's drug counselor. That gave me something to think about because he certainly didn't look like a drug counselor. I wasn't sure of any of it. But I listened to him tell me that Dave was trying to stay sober. Dave's mom had called me to let me know that Dave was seeing someone and that she didn't think she was good for him. Dave's mother was a strong German woman that you could tell loved her son. She told me she didn't like this other woman he was seeing and didn't think she was right for him. I told her there's nothing I can do about it because he and I are not a thing. But I couldn't help thinking, "Oh my god, his own mom is trying to rat him out."

DAVID ELLEFSON: I went home for Christmas, and my dad always made us go to church. I'd been going to AA meetings. I'd been through rehab three times and was working with my drug counselor, John Bocanegra, twice a week. At church with my family, the pastor delivered a message that somehow really resonated with me. I realized that everything they were talking about in AA and rehab and church was all the same message. Basically, they all said to find God and get out of trouble. Keep doing it your way, stay in trouble—that was basically the message.

DAVE MUSTAINE: We needed to move the album project along. Before we left for Christmas, we went back in the studio to cut some more demos. After "No More Mr. Nice Guy," we began working in earnest on the songs for the next album, although we still didn't have a lead guitar player. I looked and looked, but I hated everybody because they just were not good enough. They had to have attitude, they had to have appearance, and they had to have ability, and we just couldn't find anybody. I asked our old guitarist Chris Poland if he would come into the studio and help out on some demos. All he needed to do was play the solos. There was no way I was ever going to ask Chris Poland to rejoin Megadeth.

DAVID ELLEFSON: In the same building where Lippman and Kahane had their office on Sunset Boulevard, EMI Music Publishing kept a little songwriting studio. We went in to record all the songs that we had at that time, which would become *Rust in Peace*. We hired Chris Poland to come in to play some guitar solos on the tracks. He had long been out of Megadeth. He was also very much sober. We paid him cash, something like $500 per track.

RANDALL KERTZ: There was a little talk about maybe bringing Chris Poland back. He was coming around, not necessarily playing, but hanging out. There was a little kinship there.

DAVID ELLEFSON: He was sober, so I'm sure he probably wasn't too keen on being around us because we were not clean yet. We were trying to be, but we weren't yet. Obviously, that was an issue. It was after hours during the demo sessions, and Dave and I went down to Ron's office a couple of floors below in the same building at Lippman and Kahane. On his desk were albums by Cacophony and *Dragon's Kiss,* the solo album by Cacophony guitarist Marty Friedman. Dave and I knew him vaguely from a thrash-metal band called Hawaii, but his name made him sound more like a Borscht Belt comedian than a heavy metal guitar shredder. We made fun of his name, but Ron told us the guy was asking about an audition. Dave and I were like, "You know what? Fuck it. Why not? We haven't had any luck yet; what's another audition going to hurt?"

SEVEN

MARTY

DAVID ELLEFSON: By January 1990, we started planning to record, no matter what. We needed to get in the studio and make the *Rust in Peace* album. During the summer, we had auditioned a bunch of guitar players after Nick came in the band. None of them worked out. We were assuming it would be like *So Far, So Good . . . So What!*—me and Dave with our new drummer, Nick. Going into the studio with only the three of us seemed probably how we would end up doing the album. Terry Lippman from Lippman-Kahane didn't quite understand the dynamics of this, but he managed record producer Mike Clink. We certainly knew of Mike Clink from the Guns N' Roses record, which was currently the biggest-selling rock album seen in years, but Dave and I were more impressed that he had worked on the UFO album *Strangers in the Night* under Ron Nevison. That was the cool card for Mike to us.

Since Ron Laffitte had taken charge as the manager, things had stabilized. He had us at least on the road to sobriety. He had reconnected with Capitol Records. He was able to open up the recording fund to get money to make the demo, and now he was starting to put album sessions on the calendar. He brought in Mike Clink to produce. Things were starting to line up with the schedule of recording. We said, "You know what? Fuck it. Let's go rehearse. Let's try Marty." We didn't have any high hopes.

DAVE MUSTAINE: Because I had the songs and I demo'd them with Chris Poland, I didn't want to wait. I carried the brunt of the band anyway every time we went into the studio, so I didn't see any big problem. I did all the rhythm playing and we would have the other guitarists do an alternate rhythm that would go up the middle. The way we liked to mix guitars, you'd hear two guitar tracks in unison going on both outside tracks and then right up the middle, a third track. Until Marty joined the band, the other guitar players were accomplished at rhythm, but it was Marty who turned out to be fantastic at both rhythm and lead. Megadeth rhythms are extremely complex most of the time. Marty got really great at rhythm, but even he would tell you that he's a better lead player than a rhythm player. There is an art to that shit.

Finding a guitar player had proven to be nearly impossible. We had plenty of guys come and they were all different mind-sets. When David Ellefson and I were auditioning people, as soon as the audition was over, we'd reach behind our back where we had little wireless packs on our guitar straps, and turn them off. We'd go "click, click" . . . and the audition was over. One guy came in with a fluorescent Ibanez pink guitar, ready to jam. As soon as we started playing, he was off to the races. We said, "Whoa—slow down, dude. Play *with* us. You're not going to play faster than us and change the song to your tempo. You're going to play it the way that we play." We started the song again. He did it again. David and I both reached behind our backs. *Click. Click.*

Near the end of the auditions, there was one really young guitarist that came up from San Diego who argued with me in front of everyone as he was packing his gear up after his audition that he had written "Wake Up Dead." He would have had to have been ten years old when that song came out. I guess that's the closest to an occupational hazard I've ever had with my job. I looked for something, anything to click!

The last guy who came in had driven down from the Bay Area. He was a good-looking, muscular blond guy with a nice guitar and a Corvette. I pleaded with him to come down, but he kept dragging his feet. When he finally showed up, he was wearing those square-toed leather boots and was kind of a cowboy. He set up his gear, got everything ready, and looked at me—"All right, show me the songs." I thought, "Are you fucking kidding me? You're coming to an audition and you don't know one song?" *Click. Click.*

BOB NALBANDIAN: I had known Marty Friedman since 1982 when he was in the band Vixen, before his group Hawaii. When he and Hawaii came over to Los Angeles from Hawaii to do some shows, they were all staying in one room of a raggedy Sunset Boulevard motel and the shows the promoter promised them all vanished. I got them booked at a club called Radio City in Anaheim, which was a popular nightclub where Metallica and Slayer did their first gigs. I was a fanzine writer, a journalist, but I started working with him, helping him out, acting as his manager. He moved to San Francisco, where he started doing his solo stuff with Mike Varney. Varney hooked him up with Jason Becker, and they formed Cacophony. That band did the two records, and Jason left to play with David Lee Roth, and drummer Deen Castronovo went with Bad English. After Cacophony ended up falling apart, Marty was kind of frustrated. He told me he really wanted to get in a big band. He wanted to be a rock star. I landed him an audition with Ozzy Osbourne; Sharon Osbourne flew Marty down to LA. This was before they got Zakk Wylde in the band. That didn't pan out for him.

I knew Ron Laffitte and that Megadeth was looking for a guitarist. I told Ron I had a killer guitar player for them. I sent him the Cacophony CDs and Marty's solo album, *Dragon's Kiss.* Ron called back and said the music is killer, the guy could obviously play, and would fit in great—but, dude, his image. It's a little glammy, he said. He was looking at a photo shoot arranged by a record label trying to make the band look "heavy metal," but I had a more recent session that showed Marty as he was naturally, wearing torn jeans, black leather, and a Ramones T-shirt. He called back and said, "Yeah, this will work."

RANDALL KERTZ: Marty's audition day was my last day with the group. I heard them talk about Marty Friedman and nobody particularly asked for my opinion, but I was like, "Marty Friedman . . . wow!" I knew him from him being in the band Hawaii. What a great player. This could be a great thing. I answered the phone at the studio when he called that morning. I was a twenty-two-year-old heavy metal rock fan and, to me, they were all rock stars. Until they're not. He called the pay phone at the studio and told me he didn't know how to find the place and he was still waiting for his ride. I gave him the directions. He showed up about an hour later wearing battered sneakers with holes and a ragged Ramones muscle T. He was carrying his guitar—a red Carvin—and didn't even have a case. That was when I realized the reality of his rock stardom.

DAVE MUSTAINE: We videotaped all the auditions. I had this theory about interviewing people; this job was capable of destroying people and you're not going to know if it's the right person unless you see them at their weakest. We set up a video camera and recorded everything. We would just ask them random questions, and when the interview was over and the guy was gone, we would hit play and fast-forward at the same time and watch the facial expressions and body language. Everybody had these idiosyncrasies. If you don't see the tape on fast-forward, you don't see the idiosyncrasies. I even did this to my bassist, David Ellefson, and we saw where he unconsciously licked the corners of his mouth like a lizard. Under the lens of the video camera, you can pick up on those little tics. It's something I learned when I went to acting school—make sure you don't have any "tells," nothing that gives you away in every role. Like Harrison Ford always smiles with one side of his face crunched up. Every time he does it, there's that Harrison Ford smile again. I wanted to look at the videotapes and see if this Marty guy had any weird habits. I had seen his picture on his CD cover and wasn't a fan of his orange and black hair. I

RUST IN PEACE

was put off, to say the least, but we played the CD anyway and the music did the talking. At the audition, we didn't even get to the video interview with Marty because of his playing. All those weird little tricks that we were doing, trying to delouse the other applicants, kind of went out the door with Marty.

MARTY FRIEDMAN: I was borderline homeless at the time. I was crashing in a broken-down apartment at Franklin and Highland in Hollywood and living on rice and lollipops. They sold big bags of lollipops for sixty-nine cents and that was all I ate. I had an audition for Madonna the same week as Megadeth, but Megadeth was earlier in the week, so I didn't even bother going to Madonna. And no question, I liked Megadeth more than Madonna, so I was glad it worked out that way, because at that point I was just ready to go anywhere that I could get work and eat.

DAVE MUSTAINE: We were rehearsing at the Power Plant over on Sherman Way in North Hollywood, where we had finished writing the album and were tightening up everything for recording, when Marty came in. He brought his own guitar tech named Tony De-Leonardo, which impressed us. He had a real guitar tech, who set all his shit up.

MARTY FRIEDMAN: I was smart to hire a guitar tech to handle my equipment. I'm not really a gear person, so I showed up prepared with a guitar tech to set my gear up properly and make sure that it went smoothly.

72

MARTY

DAVE MUSTAINE: Marty walked in with this red Carvin guitar. Carvin instruments are notoriously inexpensive. He had a little rack mount. I think it was an ADA processor or something. No cabinets. No amplifier. A rack mount thing and a guitar. I thought, "All right, Marty, where's your amps?" I kept expecting someone to turn up with a speaker cabinet. Nothing. I told Tony, "Listen, I know you don't work for me, but I need you to do something, okay?"

I sent him to this wall I had of the most beautiful Marshall amplifiers. I told him to set up two stacks for Marty. He would use one of my stacks for his rhythm part, but when it came time for his lead solo, all he had to do was step on the button and the second stack of Marshalls would kick in. That way, I would be able to tell how the solo was.

We start playing along. Every other time we've done this audition with people, we'd be playing along and they may have gotten the rhythm close—and I figured I could fix the rhythm—but the solo was always the definitive moment. He started by playing the rhythms really well—not exact, but really well. Then the solos come in. Every other guy up until now has gone up and stepped on that transformative button, and that was the moment of truth. Would they know the solos? None of them did.

Marty got up there. I watched him in these skin-tight stretch jeans with the knees all ripped out. He was wearing high tops that weren't tied. He had a black leather jacket with a Ramones shirt. And when he stepped on the lead button, the world stopped. I knew I'd found my new guitar player.

DAVID ELLEFSON: We plugged in and Marty had learned "Wake Up Dead," "Peace Sells," maybe two or three songs. I remember we ran through "Wake Up Dead" and it was like, "Wow, that was pretty good." It wasn't perfect, but it was pretty good. He looked cool. He seemed like he understood what we were doing. He knew the parts reasonably well and he seemed hungry for the gig. By the end of the next song, it was obvious that we had finally found the guy.

MARTY FRIEDMAN: It was great. It was like we were high school friends, if we had gone to the same high school. It was really kind of a no-brainer. We were all very similar in musical taste, ambition, and musical sensibilities, and there wasn't really a whole lot that made us feel uncomfortable. It all felt very normal. I showed up and played and was friendly enough, and I thought the guys played really well.

DAVE MUSTAINE: When it was done, I reached behind my back, clicked off my cordless. Ellefson clicked off his cordless. I went outside to the Power Plant pay phones and called up my manager, Ron Laffitte. I said, "We've got our guy, except his name's Friedman and Friedman doesn't sound very metal, so we're going to have to have him change his last name." Ron told me that was not going to happen; he was an already established guitar player with several albums to his credit. I said, "Okay, Friedman it is." He was that good. I wasn't even going to argue. I went back in and I said, "You got the job, Marty. Let's start working on things." We rented him an apartment, we rented him a Mercedes-Benz, and we said go fix that hair.

MARTY

MARTY FRIEDMAN: Dave took off his guitar and said, "Don't go anywhere." I looked at Junior and said, "What does that mean?" And Junior said, "I think that means you're in the band." Apparently, they'd gone through a bunch of other guys. I heard horror stories about guys who would come in and showboat or they looked wrong or they didn't speak English or whatever. I guess they auditioned quite a few guys, but I simply showed up prepared and it was really nice. I was glad. I had hired my good friend as guitar tech that day, and he ended up getting the gig for Megadeth. I was glad I could help him because he was a really a class-A guitar tech.

DAVID ELLEFSON: After the audition, Dave pulled Marty aside and basically hired him on the spot. He said, "You know what? We're going to hire you." A few days later, Mike Clink stopped by the studio to meet us and listen to the band rehearse. The schedule was set to go into the studio and start recording the album in March.

MARTY FRIEDMAN: I was not only glad that I could eat and move out of that dump where I lived, but that I was in a band where I liked the music. Making money in music is like winning the lottery, but being in a band where you like the music is hitting the jackpot. I didn't know anything about their drug issues. I was not all that aware of that even existing in real life anyway. I was never in that world of people. When I did the audition, the band appeared solid. They were tight, good-looking guys; everybody was tan, muscular, and in good shape. We were a lean, mean machine. I thought this was great; these guys were awesome. But then, I started attending these band meetings where they had drug counselors from Alcoholics Anonymous and that was a whole new world for me. All I could think was this is what rock stars do, I guess.

DAVE MUSTAINE: During one of the talks Marty and I had when he was in the band, he told me when he was younger and lived in Maryland he used to take Quaaludes all the time and he would walk home through the snow with his shirt off. I laughed at him. He said, "Oh, dude, just wait." Then he told me before he took Quaaludes every day, he had straight hair, and once he stopped taking them, his hair went completely curly.

DAVID ELLEFSON: Marty was in the band only a couple of weeks and Dave had gone to a place called the Physicians Smoke Stop in Beverly Hills to stop smoking. Like all things with Dave, when Dave stops smoking, everybody has to stop smoking. I was smoking two packs a day like a good junkie. They finally outlawed smoking on airplanes, so I could see the end. It was like, "Oh my god, I've got to stop smoking."

Dave, Marty, and Nick drove me over to the clinic in Dave's little Mercedes E190. They warned me that the doctors at the clinic were going to give me drugs that would fuck me up and I needed to have someone drive me home. They gave me this shot in the neck behind the ear, another shot in the arm. I got really fucked up. Basically, the drugs they gave you were like Antabuse, which they use for alcoholics; if you smoked, you got sick.

They took me home and I woke up the next day in my Studio City apartment with everything fresh and clean. I'd washed all my clothes, my sheets, and everything, so I would come home to a smoke-free apartment. That night, I went to the Rainbow with my ex-girlfriend–now wife Julie. We had been estranged over the previous year or so because of my drug problems and were only reconnecting as friends, not dating or anything. She was friends with Richie Ramone, the current drummer in the Ramones at that time, and his wife, who lived not too far from me in Studio City.

At the Rainbow, everybody else was still smoking and I reached out to take a puff off someone else's cigarette. Oh my god, I had never felt so sick. As soon as the smoke hit my lungs, I felt like I was going to puke. That was the last time I smoked. Also, coming home from the Physicians Smoke Stop Clinic, I stopped taking the Buprenex stuff. I had stepped myself down to small doses, but that Physicians Smoke Stop thing helped me get over the hump of not smoking and get through the final detox off heroin. It was the last week of February, which is why I call March 1, 1990, my sobriety date. It's been my sobriety date ever since.

- EIGHT -

RUMBO

MIKE CLINK: My manager from Lippman-Kahane called and asked if I would be interested in doing a Megadeth record because their manager, Ron Laffitte, was also affiliated with the firm. I started in rehearsal. I didn't have a whole lot of time because I was so busy, and part of my agreement when I decided to do the Megadeth record was if Guns N' Roses called, I would be able to leave the project and go start on the Guns N' Roses record. The only way I could agree to do the Megadeth record was if I was able to leave if I got the call to start on that record, because obviously that was a big record. We had already done two records at that point, *Appetite* and *Lies*.

DAVID ELLEFSON: Mike Clink was hired to do the record. Terry Lippman managed him. We did not know that the only reason Mike was available was because Axl Rose was on a hiatus from recording with Guns N' Roses. We entered into the studio with Mike Clink. There really was no preproduction other than Mike Clink coming over once or twice to the Power Plant rehearsal studio in North Hollywood. The songs were written.

Despite all of our addictions and our darkest days of 1989, we somehow managed to write. Marty was kind of still learning the songs on his own, but Dave, Nick, and I had the songs down.

Mike didn't have much to do with the producing of the record from a musical point of view. His role was really to capture the band's performances and our songs to tape the way that we performed them, live in the rehearsal room. We went into Rumbo Recorders out in Canoga Park, a studio owned by the late Daryl Dragon of Captain & Tennille. Mike had done *Appetite for Destruction* with Guns N' Roses at Rumbo. It seemed a bit sleepy; there was not a lot of activity. We moved into the big room, studio A, where we cut the drums.

DAVE MUSTAINE: I thought we were booked into Rumble Studio. I was thinking, fuck yeah, we're going to rumble. But I got there and it's Rumbo? They told me this was Captain & Tennille's studio, and I immediately found that weird. I lost all respect for the place. Didn't seem like the right place to be making heavy metal. We were out near Topanga Canyon making "Hangar 18" in the "Muskrat Love" studio, and Clink showed up with his whale-tail Porsche and his puppy. He had told me if Axl calls during the recording, he would have to leave, and I thought he was out of his mind. Plus, I hate Porsches.

DAVID ELLEFSON: Dave was there with us initially. We loaded in, set up with the drums in the big room facing the control room, and stuck the bass amp in the same room so I could be standing there with Nick to play along to the songs as he recorded the drums. Dave was really struggling, being very loaded at this point, and things were not all that friendly. That transition from using drugs to sobriety can be ugly. I was newly sober, literally within a couple of weeks, and Marty was basically sitting on the couch in the control room learning the songs, working on his solos.

DAVE MUSTAINE: Marty was such a great guitar player, it caused a crisis of confidence in me. Voices inside my head starting picking on me. Going into the studio brought all these raging doubts crashing down on me. I stayed in the lounge or the kitchen, feeling discouraged about my guitar playing. Until then, I thought of myself as one of the best guitar players in the world, but here was this new guy—granted, he was really good at lead, but he was not a well-rounded player; not a rhythmic-lead-acoustic-electric-songwriter-lyric-writer-producer-engineer. He was not all these things. He was only a lead guitar player. But, in my diseased mind, he still was so much better than me that I simply crumbled. I thought, here, I've been playing all these years, and I should be so much better.

I got discouraged. I had enough disappointment and letdown in my life, with my dad never showing up and all that fucked-up kid stuff, that when that reality sank in, I just thought, "You know what? This is the one thing that gave me any kind of self-worth, and now look at me. I could have been so much better and I'm not." The voices returned, growing louder and louder—"You suck. You really do suck. You should have been kicked out of Metallica. You should have been kicked out of Megadeth, too." No wonder I relapsed.

DAVID ELLEFSON: We had seven songs, and the first thing we did was put down scratch tracks. We would write these quick tracks, which were like rough drafts or floorplans to the track. Every time we changed tempos—and the songs on *Rust in Peace* featured numerous, often radical tempo changes—we would record, stop, set the new tempo, punch it in. It was all very laborious. Dave, Nick, and I cut scratch tracks so we knew the right tempo and changes. We had only just finished that process when Dave got whisked away to detox at the Beverly Hills Medical Center. I had three weeks sober.

DAVE MUSTAINE: This time I wanted to go into treatment. I was going to come back out and meet up with those guys as soon as I could. I'm sure it probably came as a surprise to a lot of people because of my willingness to do that, because that was the first time I had truly surrendered.

DAVID ELLEFSON: Dave, Nick, Ron, and a couple of others went to see Cheap Trick at the Whiskey on Sunset. Dave fell off the wagon that night drinking. Ron and Nick told me about it the next day, and they were laughing about it. Dave can actually be pretty funny, but it was scary at the same time; when he falls, he doesn't just trip, he falls all the way. They said he was dancing-on-the-tables, ma-niacal drunk, and part of me, three weeks sober, rejoiced. Dave's off the wagon. Now I can party again too. That made me question myself: Exactly who was I sober for? Are you sober for him or are you sober for you? Because I'd gotten this threat—if you don't get clean, you're out of the band—which initially kind of drove me to sobriety out of resentment. Ironically, many years later, I have come to understand that resentment is the number one reason recovering alcoholics go out and get loaded. A year earlier, when Dave left rehab, I left. A year later, we were having the exact same experience, but this time I knew I had to fucking get through this. I had to stay sober. I had to do this for me. Dave may never get sober. Dave being my friend or not, band or no band, I have got to stay clean.

DAVE MUSTAINE: There's that threat again to get clean or get out of the band. For the record, I don't remember ever saying anything like that, and I never wanted David Ellefson to be "anything or else!" The record was almost completely written. However their stories would all change.

MIKE CLINK: I started on the record cutting the drums with Nick Menza. I would sit there with the yellow notepaper and have Nick play to a click track. I would make notes on every take that he did. Sometimes Junior would do a scratch bass track. I knew the parts, but the music was complicated by all the time changes and signature changes. I came up with a system to cut the individual sections of the songs, and I would splice the tape together later.

DAVID ELLEFSON: By then, Dave was really a mess. He could be ornery and contentious. He cut off one argument we had when I said something about something not being fair. "I don't give a fuck if it's not fair," he said. After he disappeared off to rehab, Mike Clink was the producer, the man in charge of the session, but I was now essentially the musical director. I knew what to do. I knew the marching orders and the direction we needed to go. We started to record, Nick and me in the big room wearing headphones with the scratch tracks in our ears. Of course, we knew the songs. We didn't even have to have the scratch tracks up loud in the cans. Nick and I would take three passes at each song, top to bottom, Mike would record them, and we would pick the best of those three.

The process could be quite complex. Take, for instance, "Holy Wars." That song, in particular, had at least three tempos, and sometimes, even if the tempo sounds the same, when we came to a chorus, we would speed up slightly or slow down slightly. There were a lot of nuances. Mike was recording to two-inch tape. I wondered how he could keep everything straight. He took incredible notes, and I learned what a great engineer Mike Clink is. He didn't really have to make any notes about the music. Quite honestly, I don't know if he even understood the music. He had done UFO. He did Guns N' Roses. But what we were doing with *Rust in Peace* was groundbreaking and brand-new. We were the next generation. But he knew how to record us and get our sound to tape.

Nick and I would tape each section three times and Clink would catalog it. We'd do the next section three times and he would log that. We managed about two songs a day and it took about a week to finish this part of the process. When we were done, Clink told us to take off and leave him alone for a week. He wanted to edit the tracks together. He was hanging strips of tape all around. The studio walls had two-inch tape hanging all over them. It looked like a spaghetti of Ampex tape ribbons laying around, but each one was diligently marked.

MIKE CLINK: The thing about two-inch tape is you can't see what's on the tape. Once you cut that tape, you've got to know what you're doing because it can be easy to take out eight bars of music, put the tape back together, and have it not make sense anymore. Regardless of all your notes, unless you're extremely careful, you can really screw it up. I labeled everything. I took nails and nailed all the reels of tape to the back wall of the studio, and I spent a week putting the record together. It was quite a methodical process. Once I had all the pieces together, I had Junior come in and play the bass parts. And everything worked. Not one single edit that I did, did not work.

DAVID ELLEFSON: After a week, Mike had the album edited. It had taken a week to lay down the scratches, a week to cut the drums, a week to edit it together, and now it was me playing bass and Mike Clink. We could usually cut two bass songs per day. The songs were very complex. Because my bass tone was very trebly and pointed, with a lot of clarity, there was no room for error. It needed to be executed precisely and there was obviously a lot of tempo changes. It took about a week. The last song that we recorded was "Hangar 18" and, mostly because the song is in the key of D and the bass only goes down to E, I wanted to try to find a five-string bass to record that song. Mike and I went all over looking for something suitable, but we couldn't find anything. I ended up using a four-string bass and tuning the E string down a whole step to D, recorded the front half of the song, and then tuned it up to standard tuning when we came to the back half, punched in, and recorded the rest of the song.

DAVE MUSTAINE: Finding a five-string bass at the time was difficult, but we found some great-sounding Modulus basses, and David's sound was remarkable on this album.

DAVID ELLEFSON: Every so often, Mike would stop and look up at me. "Dave coming in today?" he would ask. "No, probably not," I would say. I knew Dave was in rehab, and Mike didn't. Our thinking was to keep it away from Mike. We didn't want him getting cold feet on the session.

MIKE CLINK: I was tracking only drums and bass. But I could hear in my head exactly what the songs were going to sound like. I knew all the bits that I needed, even though I had never cut the pieces together. I had my notes. After all the tracks were done, I must have had fifty or more reels of two-inch tape, and I brought them all into studio A at Rumbo and laid them all out. It was like a garage with car parts laying everywhere. I had tapes all over the place.

Dave wasn't there for a lot of the record, but I didn't notice. I had tunnel vision when I made that record, like most records I make. I plowed through every day. I showed up at the studio and started working. I spent two weeks working on the bass and was getting ready to think about having Dave lay down his guitar parts when I realized I hadn't seen Dave in a while. When we cut the tracks, he was never in the room; he was always on the couch in the lounge. He wasn't around when we cut the drum tracks. Now I had been doing the bass with Junior for two weeks and didn't think I'd seen Dave once. I was getting ready to start recording guitars with him. "Where's Dave?" I asked Junior.

"I guess it's time to tell you," he said. "He's in rehab." You might think that could have been important information for the producer of the record. But, no. They didn't tell me because they didn't want to get me pissed off or upset. So they just didn't say anything.

Every time I had looked, Dave was sleeping on the couch. I didn't give it much thought. I had dealt with so many bands who had those kinds of problems, unless it affected my work directly, I didn't pay attention to it. He wasn't doing anything in front of me, but even the Guns N' Roses guys never did drugs in front of me. Not once. I told them from the first day that wasn't acceptable to me.

MARTY FRIEDMAN: Dave wasn't there most of the time. I found this kind of odd because he was supposed to be the Mr. Megadeth guy, but he wasn't even there. When he did show up, he asked me if I could loan him a hundred bucks. I had just joined the band after being homeless and he drives up in a Mercedes asking me for a hundred bucks. I didn't know what to make of any of this because I was quite naive. I knew that I really liked the guys, but the whole drug thing was the hardest part for me to overcome. I didn't want to go back to being homeless. I really liked the band, but I thought it was incredibly stupid that they have a band this cool and they would risk fucking it up over getting high. I guess that's the power of drugs over an addict, but I thought it was lame and embarrassing. I didn't want to tell anybody about all the AA stuff.

DAVID ELLEFSON: We put down the scratch tracks. Dave went down hard, back into smack and all the stuff. He disappeared to the Beverly Hills Medical Center. Nick and I showed up every day at Rumbo Recorders, six days a week, to lay down the drum tracks. Dave essentially was gone for the next month. He pretty much wasn't there for almost half of *Rust in Peace*.

DAVE MUSTAINE: I was so intimidated by Marty's playing that I went out and bought heroin. I was making the record of my career. I put everything together, and almost as soon as we set up the starting blocks, I took myself out of the race. Thankfully, I wrote all of the songs and did all of those demos. Here I was again, fucked up on heroin, on my way to the hospital. How did this happen again?

NINE

CUTTING GUITARS

DAVID ELLEFSON: Mike Clink kept asking, Are you sure you don't have any more songs? He always felt we were one song short from a complete album. We had done the scratches. We had cut the drums. Mike had finished the edits. We were done with bass, and we were ready for guitars, but I still had this bass riff that would become "Dawn Patrol." I laid it down and Nick put drums to it. Nick had another song called "My Creation" that he tracked. Marty took a crack at one or two takes on rhythm guitar parts. He knew he wasn't quite ready to play the rhythm guitar parts because they were highly complex with a lot of nuances in the picking. That was really Dave's specialty—his rhythm guitar playing on Megadeth; most of the sound of Megadeth comes from his right hand. I knew to play my bass parts exactly how Dave plays with his right hand. He and I are 100 percent in sync. Even though he wasn't there, I knew what to do and could lay that down.

DAVE MUSTAINE: When David and I first met, I asked him if he'd be willing to invent "lead bass guitar." He is by far the best bassist I know.

DAVID ELLEFSON: It was the week before the sessions started in March when I had gone over to Jimmy Bain's house. He had been one of my heroin buddies. He played bass for Ronnie Dio and loaned me an eight-string bass. I took it home to my apartment in Studio City and came up with the bassline that became "Dawn Patrol." I played it until my fingers hurt. My mind was filled with doubts because I was newly sober. Do I even want to play bass any longer, I wondered. Instantly, my mind snapped back. "You have been playing bass since you were eleven years old," the voice in my head spoke. "You started taking drugs when you were fifteen, and the drugs have been in the way the entire time. They never enhanced anything." It was this voice-of-God moment where this thought came to me, and I knew with complete certainty that I do like the bass and I do want to do this. That thought was powerful enough to start me falling in love again with playing bass and being in a band.

MIKE CLINK: With Dave missing in action, I didn't skip a beat. I went on with Marty. I originally planned to do Dave first and then Marty, but went ahead with Marty and figured I would do Dave when he came back. I brought in my assistant from the Guns N' Roses *Appetite* sessions, Micajah Ryan.

CUTTING GUITARS

MICAJAH RYAN: When I came in on the sessions, the drums and bass had already been recorded. I came in for the guitars. I met Mike when I worked as an assistant engineer at a studio called Take One, which is where the *Appetite for Destruction* overdubs were done. We spent three months doing those overdubs, and then we worked together on *Lies*. He called and I went over to his house. He told me he needed me to help out with the Megadeth sessions because he had other projects looming. He asked me to come in and help him with the guitars. Before that, I had only been an assistant engineer; I hadn't really done any first engineering. When I came to work with Mike, we started with Marty. Mike began working on getting a guitar sound for Marty.

MARTY FRIEDMAN: To be honest with you, Clink wasn't really there that much during the guitars, but when he was, he was very useful, and I was on cloud nine. Clink had just produced the biggest rock album of all time, *Appetite for Destruction*. A couple of months earlier, I had been fanning my balls on Franklin Avenue, and now I was with the top producer in the world. He was super. He made me feel comfortable with casual comments, little things to think about when I was playing. He always said the right thing that pointed me in the right direction. But the majority of it was myself and Micajah and a guitar tech. There wasn't a whole lot of creative direction when it came to my guitar parts. I pretty much was left to do what I wanted.

DAVE MUSTAINE: Remember, Chris Poland had already laid down solos on the *Rust in Peace* demos.

MARTY FRIEDMAN: I had other problems that I couldn't let anybody know about. I had a serious arm issue, far worse than tendonitis. The nerves on my right arm had become detached and were mangled inside, barely connected to each other enough to have the synapse from my brain get to my hands. If I shook someone's hand, it would feel like a big electric shock going through my arm. I had just joined a band on a major label, and I didn't want anybody to know about it. I had a doctor tell me to quit playing guitar or I could lose use of my arm entirely. He did not understand that I was recording this album. I went for a second opinion from a sports medicine doctor, and she said the first doctor was probably right, but she knew I was not going to stop playing at this point and worked to minimize the injury. I went to therapy every day for a couple of months. The doctor recommended I only play the barest minimum; no warming up, no noodling around, do as few takes as possible, just record when the red light is on, get your shit done, and get out of there. That is totally not my style. I like to do a lot of takes. I like to live with things and think about what I'm playing, try stuff and change things. But no, she said, play as little as possible.

That was what I did. I would often have to wear a kind of sling for my arm when I wasn't playing. To cover up the fact that I was wearing this sling, I wore a sweatshirt, which is weird in LA in the daytime. Eventually, I couldn't keep it secret any longer because I had to ice my arm. I needed to let them know that I was going to be icing my arm because it looks crazy. I didn't tell them how serious it was, and they didn't ask; guitarists are always doing strange things with their hands and fingers. But the main thing that was in my mind was play as little as possible, get the stuff done right the first time, don't linger around; get in and get out.

I don't think it affected my playing very much. It meant that I wasn't able to get into the minutiae of fixing little details. My previous album with Cacophony was in-depth, guitar-intensive, extremely modern, unorthodox, and highly technical unusual Philip Glass– and Stravinsky-influenced things, complex music that required a lot of attention to detail. Luckily, in Megadeth, it was closer to pop music in structure—verse, chorus, and solo— and not one of these big, orchestrated guitar extravaganzas that needed a lot more attention. It was really about capturing energy, and usually you capture the best energy in the first couple of takes anyway. In the end, I wasn't dissatisfied with anything, although it would have been nice to have a more fun environment for my first major album.

MICAJAH RYAN: Clink got the sound for Marty and from then on it was pretty much left up to me to record all the guitars. I came into this thing cold. I knew very little about Megadeth. I wasn't a metal person and knew next to nothing about heavy metal. I didn't know anything about what was going on with the band. Marty was so new to the band he didn't know always what he was supposed to do. He would have to call Dave in rehab in the morning and ask how a song was supposed to go. Marty might have had an idea, but he needed to check with Dave in rehab.

DAVE MUSTAINE: The first time I went into rehab, I had no idea what to expect. This time was different; I was a rehab veteran. I knew this was basically go in, get detoxed, go back to work. By now, I knew what I was doing. I knew all the medical terms. I knew all the medications. I knew that I was probably going to be anemic because I'd been eating a lot of candy. I knew that I would probably need something for my blood pressure, probably Klonopin or clonidine. I knew that I would need some kind of antianxiety medication, like Versed, which is liquid valium, or something like Vistaril. They would start working on the detox, however long that took. Bocanegra was there to make sure everything went smooth. As soon as that was over, I went back to the studio and I got to work.

DAVID ELLEFSON: A month later, Dave came out of rehab. We had moved to studio C and I watched in some amazement as he started work on "Holy Wars." He hadn't played guitar in a month, and the last time he'd played, he was high. Warming up, he was a little rusty. He always recorded stereo, one track to the left and then a second track to the right, doubling the part. Once he started filling up the tracks, he was flying. Hearing it come down, you could feel the emotion. In fact, there's a little bit of feedback toward the end of the song, and it was a raw moment where you could feel his intensity.

DAVE MUSTAINE: I did the solo for "Holy Wars" in one take. That is our most popular, thrashiest song and probably one of my best solos ever, and I don't know why we kept that solo. We had heard from Angus Young of AC/DC that he gets his guitar tone by having his Marshalls turned to ten and pushed up against a wall with microphone in between. It makes this ungodly bellowing. When

CUTTING GUITARS

I tried it, the guitar groaned like it was being tortured. I started playing and there were a couple of dead notes, and obviously the part where the feedback came in is not too desirable, but the solo turned out great. I figured it would be an outtake.

MIKE CLINK: Even though I pieced the record together, they were amazing players. I mean, fuck, to watch Mustaine play those rhythm parts with such accuracy, and to hear Nick Menza play all those time changes, and Junior, as fast as he would pick, I was amazed that people could play like that. This was a constant attack of notes coming at you, lickety-split. Marty was so melodic and it came to him so effortlessly. Every solo was a guitar lesson for me. Even with the speed, he really had all of those solos underneath his fingers. He had to practice, of course, but he was like a great skier going down the hill as if it was effortless. I felt the same way about his solos.

DAVID ELLEFSON: The first song Dave sang was "Holy Wars," and, again, the last time he sang the song he had been using drugs. Now he was out of rehab, maybe still a little shaky, and he comes out and starts singing. His voice was kind of thin and scratchy, but it was also surly and commanding. My first reaction was that I hoped that was a warmup take, but we ended up keeping that vocal. And that it became the first vocal you hear on *Rust in Peace* was no simple twist of fate. As I look back on it, it captured the entire essence of where we were at that exact moment, this masterpiece that we had created in the darkness of heroin and were now re-cording freshly sober.

MIKE CLINK: When Dave first got back from rehab, he was bursting with energy. Our daily schedule started around ten in the morning, when Junior and I would play tennis. We would start our sessions around eleven o'clock or noon. When Mustaine came back from rehab, the first thing he wanted to know was if we could start the sessions at eight a.m. I told him that wasn't going to happen. Even if I wasn't playing tennis, and happened to be awake at eight in the morning because I have kids, I'm not ready to start making a fucking heavy metal record at that hour. He agreed not to disrupt everything. But he was up. He had the energy and he was ready to go. I think he wanted to make up for lost time. Maybe at rehab they had him up early in the morning and he was used to that schedule, and ten o'clock or eleven o'clock might have been halfway through his day, but he didn't make an issue of it, and we continued our usual schedule.

- TEN -

AXL CALLS

MIKE CLINK: We were four-fifths of the way done with the record when Axl called. We had a couple solos and a couple vocals to do. It wasn't like I left the next day; there was a transitional period. But I was going to produce *Use Your Illusion* for Guns N' Roses; it was already certain to be a very big record.

DAVE MUSTAINE: I was goofing around in the rear of Rumbo Studios when Clink pulled in the rear parking lot as we were loading in some gear and dropped the Axl bomb on us that he'd have to leave soon.

DAVID ELLEFSON: As we were well into the recording of *Rust in Peace*, Axl suddenly says, "I'm ready to go; let's work." And that's when

Mike got pulled off the *Rust in Peace* record to go do *Use Your Illusion I* and *II*.

MIKE CLINK: They wanted to bring someone in to hear the material, listen to the tracks. Dave Jerden was brought in to mix the record. I love Dave's work. I listened to the first Jane's Addiction record and thought, "No matter how good I get, I'll never be that good." That was how I felt about that record. I thought he would be a great person to finish the record. He was there for two and a half days, sitting in a chair getting to know the band, and it just didn't work out with Dave for a couple of reasons.

MICAJAH RYAN: Dave Jerden was supposed to produce the record. He lasted about four days. Dave Mustaine came up to me and said there's too many guys named Dave around here.

DAVE MUSTAINE: We all have our own recollection of how long Jerden was around. But he was hired for the project and he was in the studio for, like, fifteen minutes before I fired him. I walked into the control room and Clink and Jerden were there. They were going to be a team and make the record together. It would have been unprecedented. But I walked in the control room and Jerden was sitting there, smoking cigarettes, eating a chili dog, and the studio smelled like a bar. It stank. I don't smoke cigarettes and this was not the way to start a project, coming in the control room and taking it over. I went, "Fuck that, I am not going to tolerate this." I told him he was through and he left. I never saw the guy again, which is too bad because Jerden is a great and talented producer.

MIKE CLINK: We were looking for someone to mix the record and Dave Jerden was brought in. But his personality and where he was in his life at that moment didn't make him the candidate to mix the Megadeth record. But I had brought in Micajah Ryan to assist me on that record. I had used him for several records, and I knew that he could get the job done. He wasn't really a producer, but he was a good finisher. Quite honestly, there wasn't that much left to do and he was perfectly suited to do it. We had spent months working together on other records, so it seemed like a natural fit.

MICAJAH RYAN: They kind of dumped it in my lap. There wasn't anybody there except me. Mike Clink got the sound for Marty, and from then on, it was pretty much left up to me. I recorded all the guitars for both Marty and Dave and then the vocals and all the background vocals until everything was done, everything was recorded.

DAVID ELLEFSON: Mike had long presented to Dave that we needed another song for the record and played him the two things that Nick and I had put down. For whatever reason, Dave liked what I had done with the bass part and wrote lyrics to it that became "Dawn Patrol." I thought it was cool that the ballad of *Rust in Peace* was created on the bass. At this point, Dave and I didn't really know how to be friends. We didn't know how to get along. Newly sober, we could almost be worse than when we were loaded, because when we were loaded, we had sort of an ointment to put over our emotions. Now, not loaded, how do we behave? What do we do with these feelings? Do we say this? Is what I'm about to say going to cause more problems? I'm probably a little bit more filtered; Dave, not so much. He and I got into a heated argument around "Dawn Patrol." I often wondered if he maybe didn't put "Dawn Patrol" on the record as a kind of olive branch of friendship to me. I don't know. I, for sure, think it was the right choice and the right song.

MICAJAH RYAN: When everybody left, when Dave Jerden left, when Dave Mustaine left and Mike Clink left, it was just me and Marty. We were working on guitar overdubs for these songs, and I didn't know the songs at all, either. I really didn't have much background in metal. But I was a guitar player, and guitars are guitars. They all have six strings and you have to put your fingers on the neck the same way. I knew about guitars. Doing these overdubs was something that I felt like I could handle. But it was crazy. I was kind of thrown into a pit and told, "Here you go. Do the best you can." There was no input from outside. I had to go by my best instincts, whatever instincts those were.

MARTY FRIEDMAN: I did a solo on "Holy Wars." Clink was there that day and liked what I did. I hated it, but who was I to argue with him? It kept bugging me. I would call Dave. I would call Junior. I called Clink. Every one of them liked the solo. I was the only one who didn't like this solo. But I became such a pain in the ass about this to everybody that they allowed me to recut it. I did and that was the one that was kept, so I was finally satisfied with everything on the record. I have had producers who were not as scrupulous with my guitar playing as I am. There can be all kinds of matters I don't like; tuning issues, phrasing issues, things that I wouldn't want to leave for posterity. It is usually smarter to go with a producer than to be an asshole guitarist. It all depends on the importance of the producer, the importance of the session, and my rank in whatever that particular scenario is. But, at that point, it was kind of ballsy for me to go in there and keep asking the producer many times to fix it. They let me, and I'm glad that they left it.

MICAJAH RYAN: We didn't hear from Mike. He was up to his neck in Guns N' Roses. He was really busy with them. Though I didn't see him or hear from him, he was supportive. The checks kept coming through and everything kept going. The project kept flowing, but there just wasn't a lot of interaction.

DAVE MUSTAINE: No offense to Mike, he's a good cat, and a great producer, but he acted like he was the only grownup in the room during this thing. He fucking left. In the middle of a project. As you sort through the details, it quickly becomes obvious that no one person was responsible for this thing happening. Some people have more contributions than others, but even as much as I want to take credit for my part in it, I know that it was a cast of players.

MICAJAH RYAN: Mike called and told me that he'd hired Max Norman to mix the record and that I had to deliver the tapes to Max at this studio called the Grey Room, which is where I'd been an assistant, so I knew that room really well. Max, of course, was the British record producer well known for the first two Ozzy Osbourne records, *Blizzard of Ozz* and *Diary of a Madman*. I took the tapes over there and walked Max through the tapes, told him what was going on, and left him to mix it. I went back to my house, waiting for my next job, and one day the phone rang, and it was Max. He said he couldn't reach anybody to approve the mixes and would I mind coming down and giving them a listen. I said I would. I tried to reach people on the project but couldn't get hold of anybody either.

DAVE MUSTAINE: After Mike left, it was just me and Micajah. Max didn't show up until the record was done and it was time to be mixed. I basically had said, "Goodbye, Mike, hello, Micajah; goodbye, Micajah, and hello Max." I don't remember if those guys were ever in the same room together with me.

MAX NORMAN: I went over to Rumbo Recorders to talk to Mike Clink. Next to studio A there was a billiard room and I walked in there. Dave was shooting pool with David Ellefson. Clink came walking in and they called him Mild Mike or Mellow Mike. Practically the first thing he said to me was there were no points. I looked at him and said okay. He laid out the deal; he had to do this thing with Guns N' Roses. Megadeth was nearly done here and simply need somebody to sort this out.

We basically agreed that it was for a fee. I had worked at One on One Studios in North Hollywood a few times, so we booked that studio. They have a small mix room on the right-hand side as you walk into the studio. We went in there and started mixing. I would work throughout the day and Dave would show up in the late afternoon. He would take a listen, make a few comments, and we would work through things.

DAVE MUSTAINE: Working with Max, we were doing things that we'd never done before. I would never have known to have recorded a cymbal, slow it down, and flip it upside down. We did that between two songs. When "Rust in Peace" ended and the second part of that song, "Polaris," started, in the middle, we hit a cymbal and slowed it down. Because if you listen to "Over the Mountain" from Ozzy's first record, there's this cymbal that sounds like a sizzle that turns into a shower and then the song starts. I asked Max what that was, and he said he hit a cymbal and slowed it down on the tape. I thought what would be really cool is to do that backwards and have it grow louder. We stuck that right in front of where the riff comes in for "Polaris."

MICAJAH RYAN: I don't know where Dave was. I didn't see him. After we finished doing the guitar overdubs and the vocal overdubs, I don't remember. The next time I saw him again was at the very end, when he had a couple things that he needed Max to do, like he wanted a backwards cymbal thrown in, just a couple little things like that. That was the only time I saw him was during the mixing, just a very little bit at the end of the process. That was the last time I saw Dave.

MAX NORMAN: Dave thought I knew all these old-school tricks to sort out the edits, of course, and he mentioned something about backwards cymbal. I was doing a lot of records at that time, and I'm sure that we did a few of those tricks, flipped the tape over and ran the tape backwards and recorded reverse reverberation and stuff like that. Those things were all pretty standard stunts in those days.

MICAJAH RYAN: Mike had recorded the drums, and he cut from different takes so he would use this part of the drums from this take, and then the next part of the drums would be from another take, and there would be a difference sonically between the drums, like the snare drum could be different in the first take, and when it went to the next take, it had a slightly different sound. Max had to spend a lot of time EQing the drums so that they sounded the same as it played back through the edits.

MAX NORMAN: Mike was very fond of doing edits, and there was quite a lot of edits on the twenty-four-track. This became apparent to me when I would be doing a playback, listening to the mix, and when it would go into a pre-chorus, the snare would totally disappear. I quickly realized that this snare was actually totally different from the one that was in the verse, probably different takes or maybe simply not being hit as well or perhaps recorded at a slightly different level. That took a lot of repair, patch into another track, automate that switchover, and then requeue for the pre-chorus. There was quite a lot of that. It took a while to stabilize the tracks. Fortunately, it only really affected the drums. It wasn't too much of a hassle, but we did spend a considerable amount of time normalizing everything all the way through the songs.

MICAJAH RYAN: I went down to the studio and Max played me the mix. I listened and said something like "I think it needs a little more drum here" and "this guitar needs to be a little louder, maybe a little more vocal here"—only little tiny tweaks. Max did that and we waited for someone else to listen to the mix to approve it, but there wasn't anybody, and we simply moved on and went through the whole record. Max was great. His mixing skills were amazing, and I was very impressed. We went through it that way until we got to the end of the record, and that was it.

- ELEVEN -

THE SONGS

HOLY WARS . . . THE PUNISHMENT DUE

The day after we played Antrim in Northern Ireland and I made my uninformed comments from the stage about "The Cause," we went to play Nottingham Rock City in England and I started writing the lyrics to "Holy Wars." It became one of our biggest songs. In fact, we close our shows with it. We used to use it to open our shows until Vinnie Paul, the drummer from Pantera, suggested we open with "Hangar 18." That sounded like a good idea to me, so we moved "Holy Wars" to the end, where it always seals the deal. The first verse came straight out of my experience at Antrim:

> *Brother will kill brother spilling blood across the land*
> *Killing for religion, something I don't understand*
> *Fools like me who cross the sea and come to*
> * foreign lands*
> *Ask the sheep for their belief*
> *Do you kill on God's command?*

Then I invoke the prophecy from the Bible in which some people believe that peace will come to Israel on all four sides before the Antichrist and the Messiah return.

> *The end is near, it's crystal clear, part of the*
>   *master plan*
> *Don't look now to Israel, it might be your*
>   *homeland Holy Wars.*

Yeah, it might be your homeland, right here in Ireland. In the middle part of the song, I step up on my soapbox, talking about the different types of people who try to indoctrinate and brainwash us with propaganda—the judge, the pastor, the salesman, the know-it-all scholar, the executioner, all these things. At this point, the song stops and the next portion of the song starts, a little break, setting up the second half of the song, "The Punishment Due." This was me writing through the lens of Frank Castle from "The Punisher," a Marvel Comics anti-hero I loved. He is this assassin and he is unrepentant. His fierce indifference—to his employers and enemies alike—makes him immune to their judgments. And it all leads to a climactic conclusion. I start with what they did to Frank Castle to harden his heart:

> *They killed my wife and my baby*
> *With hopes to enslave me*
> *First mistake, last mistake!*
> *Paid by the alliance, to slay all the giants*
> *Next mistake, no more mistakes*

That last line explodes every time in concert. The front rows of fans have their heads bobbing up and down, mouthing the words until *Next mistake, no more mistakes.* That serves as the song's punch line, and the guitar calisthenics take off from there. This song contains considerable complexity in the guitar work. It's almost like a polyphonic rhythm, where the rhythm alone is difficult enough, but doing the playing and singing at the same time is the musical equivalent of rubbing your belly and patting your head. Not easy.

You never know where a song comes from or where it is going to go. A lot of times, they start off with totally different tempos. "Holy Wars" began life much slower. Once we got it into the studio, we sped it up considerably.

The video was important to the song's success. We had a big video for this song. Directed by Benjamin Stokes and Eric Zimmerman, two video producers from Chicago we used to call Bert and Ernie. The video turned out great, I thought, except for one minor detail. We got enough grief from people making fun of us for playing with our shirts off, but when the little toy tank comes in during the middle and shoots a puff of smoke out of the cannon, I was beside myself. That was about the dumbest thing I ever saw, and I told Bert and Ernie to take it out. I was furious when I saw they left it in. Apparently, someone's girlfriend made the damn thing, so the toy tank stayed in the video.

Almost above all others, that song has a special place in our fans' hearts. To this day, whenever somebody puts a guitar in my hands to sign, I will pick out the opening riff to "Holy Wars" and tell them what I played. Always works. It's like our "Detroit Rock City."

HANGAR 18

People often compare "Hangar 18" to "Call of Ktulu" off the Metallica album *Ride the Lightning*. It does have the same chord structure, although the chords are not played in the same sequence. But since I wrote both songs, it stands to reason they use the same chords. It's not played the same, but it is very similar to "Call of Ktulu," which started off life as "When Hell Freezes Over."

But "Hangar 18" has been around even longer. Before Metallica, I had been in a band called Panic, and we had played this song, but back then it was called "N2RHQ." I had been at an airport where I saw a tailfin on a plane with the number "N2RHQ." I thought that's "into our headquarters." How cool. It inspired me to write a song about a destination in outer space, our headquarters in space.

> *Welcome to our fortress tall*
> *Take some time to show you around*
> *Impossible to break these walls*
> *For you see the steel is much too strong.*
> *Computer banks to rule the world*
> *Instruments to sight the stars*

It was that whole *Tron/Star Wars/Star Trek* thing. Hangar 18 wasn't in the song at first, but it had everything except that tag line.

> *Possibly I've seen too much*
> *Hangar 18, I know too much.*

We were listening to a lot of comedy tapes back then, and I loved George Carlin and his oxymorons—jumbo shrimp, military intelligence, business ethics—which is where I lifted the line about military intelligence.

After that second verse in "Hangar 18," it was time to get down with the guitar playing. I had been watching a commercial on TV for the US Navy that showed a submarine and the sailors inside going through their paces, with a bit of music running underneath. The riff had a kind of cool energy that really struck me. I picked up my guitar and started playing around until I came up with the second half of "Hangar 18," where the guitar solo comes in.

Once we got to the solo part and started swapping off solos, it went Marty, Marty, me, Marty, me, Marty, me. And as we kept passing the baton back and forth, exchanging punches or whatever you want to call it, going back and forth between us with the solos, I decided we should speed up the song as we went along. At the end of each solo, there was a phrase following which we would bump up the tempo every time. The next time we hit each solo section, the beats per minute had picked up considerably.

TAKE NO PRISONERS

I had been watching a lot of World War II movies and the whole militant mentality of the metal world struck me as weirdly parallel. That kind of thinking had really started to invade the top ranks of the big four. It was becoming the metal militia. It was also about the same time that Tom Cruise starred in the movie *Born on the Fourth of July* about the crippled Vietnam veteran Ron Kovic.

Also, I had always looked up to President John F. Kennedy, even though I was two years old when he was killed. By the time I was a teenager and had lived through Nixon, Ford, and Carter, and it was time to register for the Selective Service, a friend and

I went to the post office together and put each other's draft registration cards in the mailbox to make sure we did it. I was skeptical about foreign wars—what was it, Korea, that was threatening at that point?—and indifferent about politics. But I knew eighteen-year-olds were piloting these billion-dollar aircraft carriers, commanding the ship, and still toeing the line. It occurred to me that these kids could sacrifice their lives, but still had to cut their hair.

I'd already witnessed the treatment the Veterans Administration gave my dad, who was an army vet. I had seen how a lot of these guys came back zombies, especially Vietnam vets, who returned to be spit on. No parades for them.

But really the song was about World War II and defeating the Third Reich. Even though my mom was German, I'm not anti-Semitic at all, so I don't think that was where I was going with this. To me, it was kind of like watching World War II go down.

> *Got one chance, infiltrate them*
> *Get it right, exterminate them*
> *The Panzers will permeate them*
> *Break their pride, denigrate them*
> *And their people, retrograde them*
> *Typhus, deteriorate them*
> *Epidemic, devastate them.*
> *Take no prisoners, cremate them*
> *Burn*

I wanted the opening to sound like a drill sergeant barking out orders, like R. Lee Ermey as Gunnery Sergeant Hartman in *Full Metal Jacket*. I had the band and myself do a gang vocal, call and response. I picked up "war is peace" from *1984* by George Orwell.

DAVE MUSTAINE AND ANDY SOMMERS
Here I am with our first booking agent, Andy Sommers. Andy believed in us, and he was heavily involved in our success.

BOB NALBANDIAN
Bob was "well connected" in the LA scene. He introduced us to Marty, and Bob is still one of the band's oldest and truest friends.

CHUCK BEHLER

Chuck, somewhere on tour. Chuck was the most punk rock of all our drummers. This was taken shortly after waking up and about to sound check. I still stay in touch with him, and we see him each time we go to Detroit.

DAVE MUSTAINE, TONY LETTIERI, AND ROMMEL

Tony was my bodyguard during this era. That is the world-famous Rommel, the Rottweiler I got for Tony and nearly missed connecting with my amazing Pam.

NICK MENZA

Nick behind the famous Megadeth Drum Set and Riser and his Yamaha
Rust in Peace drum kit.

DAVE MUSTAINE—LIVE
On stage. Temperature is rising. Optimal fitness level. Ready to take on the world.

MEGADETH—SKYDIVING

Marty made a deal with me once that if we had a record go gold, he would come dive. As you can see in this photo, he is not amused.

MEGADETH—ARENA

This is the four of us in an empty arena after one of the dates on the Clash of the Titans Tour.

DAVID ELLEFSON

David Ellefson goofing around backstage before the set. I think this had something to do with the rockumentary *This Is Spinal Tap* and the "metal detector" scene.

DAVID ELLEFSON—LIVE

David Ellefson was always upbeat and happy, and he is a fan favorite. I'm so glad we are still making Megadeth music together. Here is my friend of nearly forty years, laying down the groove.

MARTY

Marty ripping a solo, probably to "Tornado of Souls."

MEGADETH

We had the ultimate leather jackets made for the *Rust in Peace* cycle. I don't know what ever happened to mine.

DAVE MUSTAINE AND ROB HALFORD

Rob and I with our motorcycles for a magazine shoot in Arizona on a day off.

OUR *RUST IN PEACE* SET

We had attempted stage props at our first shows, but it wasn't until the *RIP* album, when this new stage setting and drum rack was made, that we looked as good as we played.

RIP BALLOONS

Epic New Year's Eve show at the Long Beach Arena.

"HANGAR 18" VIDEO SHOOT

Here we are performing at the "Hangar 18" video shoot with some fans underneath us. Look closely and see the barricade that we were up against. It looked out into a massive pit which was at least 60 feet down.

PAM MUSTAINE
Pamela Anne Casselberry, before we met and I proposed. It wasn't long after we met that we got married and settled down.

MUSTAINE WEDDING PARTY IN HAWAII
Left to right: Todd Casselberry, Ron Lafitte, David Ellefson, John Bocanerga, Dave and Pam, Julie Foley, Helen Mayhue, Stephanie Hardy.

RANDY KERTZ
Randy was David Ellefson's minder during this album cycle. He's still a really great friend of the band and has become a successful doctor in the Detroit area.

MARTY
Marty Friedman warming up before the show. He made playing look effortless.

DM LIVE

This is another photo from Gene Kirkland. We were an impenetrable circle. You were either in or you were not. Gene traveled with us a lot, was in the circle, and was the closest thing to "band photographer."

MEGADETH—END OF SHOW

These are my brothers. We will always have our ups and downs, like brothers do. There is no denying what we did for music and our fans did for us. "You've been great, we've been Megadeth."

DAVE AND DAVID

The sole survivors. We kept pushing forward against all odds, again and again, and there were many! Wait 'til you see what's NEXT!

IN MEMORY OF NICK MENZA (1964–2016)

In loving memory of Nick Menza. He was a beautiful man, an incredibly talented musician, who was my friend and brother. It was an honor to share the stages of the world with you. You made me happy, and you made me mad. We loved, we lived, and we thrashed the planet. I wept when you left us back here above ground. I know I will see you again one day. I love you and I miss you.—Dave Mustaine

THE SONGS

I vamped on the TV commercial for the army reserves that promised you could "be all that you could be" by joining the army. And finally, I hit on the John F. Kennedy line.

> *Don't ask what you can do for your country*
> *Ask what your country can do for you*
> *Take no prisoners, take no shit*

The riffing in this song makes "Take No Prisoners" one of the most complex songs on *Rust in Peace*. The beginning explodes at a breakneck pace—probably as fast as I could play that riff at the time—and it's almost like a Chinese finger puzzle. The fingering is incredibly intricate, but it is the way you do the pattern, not how fast you play it. If you do it too fast, you lose the rhythm. There's a way to do it right where there's a beautiful flow, and I couldn't get it any faster anyway. There are snappy military parts with cadences on snares and some easy rhythms, then quick left turns into fierce solos. Fans love to sing the part at the end where I say "take no prisoners, take no shit"—we always say that a bunch of times. It has always been a watchword with me. When people ask for my advice in life, I've always said don't take shit from anyone.

FIVE MAGICS

I was living at the studio in Vernon. I had built a loft and put a mattress and an overhead light up there. I had a heating element and a tin cup, where I could boil water and make up hot toddies and stuff. Sometimes I would climb in the loft with a girl, and sometimes I would sleep at their apartment, but often I would simply read at night before I went to sleep. It was a lonely time for me.

One woman used to buy heroin from a dealer I knew. I would occasionally go with her to score, and do a little bit. She would go all warm and fuzzy, and we would go to her house and spend the night. When she got up and went to work the next morning, she always told me what time I had to leave so I wouldn't be there when her roommate woke up. I would get up, make myself a cup of coffee, and leave by the time she wanted me to leave.

That was where I found the book *Master of the Five Magics*, and it fascinated me. Written by Lyndon Hardy and published in 1980, the fantasy novel, first of a trilogy, follows the adventures of Alodar in the land of Procolon as he seeks to distinguish himself sufficiently to earn the hand in marriage of Queen Vendora.

I read the book, and I'm not a plagiarist, but the book influenced me considerably. I didn't even use the same five magics; I made up my own. The song is basically a combination of that book and the 1981 movie starring Rutger Hauer and Michelle Pfeiffer, *Ladyhawke*, a romantic fantasy involving dark magics and evil enchantments. But the song starts off much like the book, with our hero looking for these powers.

Now, one part comes from the book, the wyvern, and that's the only thing I lifted directly—*parade the gray-robed monks and the vestal virgins, wheel the wyverns in.* It doesn't have anything to do with anything. I thought it sounded kind of cool.

> *Bestow upon me knowledge*
> *Wizard, all-knowing, all-wise*
> *I want to rule my kingdom*
> *Make sweet the breeze, once defiled*
> *Dethrone the evil prince's iron fists in velvet*
> * gloves of sin*

THE SONGS

Parade the grey-robed monks, the vestal virgins
Wheel the wyverns in.

Even though these five things are all individual, they're all the same. They're all magics, but they're all different. They're similar, but they're not. By the end of the song, there is a weird sing-along part where I hold a call and answer with the wizard:

Possessed with hellish torment (possessed with
*   hellish torment)*
I master magics five (I master magics five)

I don't know who he is. I never said who the wizard was, if it was a good wizard, if it was a bad one. But then you hear his voice. I wanted to get this grotesque sound effect. We tried a bunch of electronic effects, and then I simply cupped my hands and spoke into my hands, and there was this perfectly evil, hellish sound effect. That was my little evil dude—my hands. There was my evilness.

Every time I sing the song, I picture him talking to Merlin. I don't know why I didn't come out and name him—I probably did in the first draft—but I didn't.

He who lives by the sword will surely also die.
He who lives in sin will surely live the lie.

Notice after he goes *he who lives in sin*, he's waiting, and when I say, *will surely live the lie*, there's no answer. Why is there no answer? Is he the bad guy and I am the good guy now? I've got the five magics and I'm hunting the abyss lord, so obviously I'm a good guy, but who am I talking to? Is it even me? Is it Narcissus? Is it an echo? What is it? I don't wanna be some fucking overly moral dude, but I do dig Aesop and how he always put a good ending to his fables. I did not want people to think there was anything good about black magic—that stuff wrecked my life for many years. People knew that I did witchcraft, but that's something I never wanted to be popular.

POISON WAS THE CURE

I thought I knew what this song was about. At least I thought I knew. But when I looked back, it occurred to me that I'd written a metaphor for heroin and not my relationships.

> *I miss the warm embrace I felt*
> *First time you touched me*
> *Secure and safe in open arms*
> *I should have known you'd crush me*

Anyone who has ever done heroin knows that's what it feels like.

> *A snake you were when me met*
> *I loved you anyway*
> *Pulling out your poisoned fangs*
> *The venom never goes away*

That was about getting to the point where I was bit by heroin or an individual. At this point, I couldn't tell you which one the song was about. In the end, I finally regain my conscience. If you looked over all my songs, you would see that most of my songs start off with the protagonist facing adversity, but by the final chorus has overcome his enemies and emerged victorious. There is always a moral to the story; that's the Aesop's fables thing again.

> *From a rock star to a desk fool was my destiny,*
> *someone said*
> *Life's a tidepool, taste the waters, life's abundant*

That last line was something that came from my drug counselor Bocanegra, *life's a tidepool, taste the water.* He was a great influence on me getting and staying sober, but he was not a songwriter. He came to me and Ellefson once and said that he had written some lyrics he wanted us to see. It was kind of sad. I didn't want to say anything about it to him, and I am not sure if he was kidding around, but he wrote "the moon behind the clouds is so big." I told him, "Don't write lyrics. Just stay a counselor."

LUCRETIA

"Lucretia" is the subject of much controversy. People want to know who Lucretia is. They tell me I spelled her name wrong. They have all sorts of opinions about this song, but they are all wrong. I wrote this song about some make-believe thing in my head and I named her Lucretia. I don't even know who this is. I made it all up and I can spell her name any way I want to.

> *Sitting up, late at night*
> *I tiptoe through the darkness*

Cold as hell, black as spades
Aware of my immediate surrounding
In my place I escape up into my hideout
Hiding from everyone
My friends all say,
"Dave you're mental anyway"
Hey!

I could remember when I was sneaking through the houses, getting loaded, how my life had sunk to such a level of debauchery and hiding stuff from everybody. I was also reminded of my loft at the studio that was a place where I could escape up into my hideout, hiding from everyone. And then it says:

Drift into a deeper state
I stalk the cobwebbed stairways
Dirt grits between my feet
The stair creaks, I precariously sneak

That's me falling asleep and going into that place where you drift off into the twilight. It goes:

Hypnosis guides my hand
I slip-slide through the walkways
Sit in granny's rocking chair
Memories are whirling by, yeah
Reminiscing in the attic
Lucretia waits impatiently
Cobwebs make me squint
The cobra so eloquently glints

THE SONGS

When I was young, the comedian Jonathan Winters had a television show where he would go up into his attic and explain all the shit he had up there. I suppose it was some kind of physical representation of the buildup inside of his brain. One of the things he had was a stuffed snake. I pictured myself being up there in this attic with all of this crazy shit and a stuffed snake, a stuffed mongoose, the two of them sitting across from each other, a crystal ball between them. I finished this off:

> *Moonbeams surge through the sky*
> *The crystal ball's energized*
> *Surely that like the cat waiting*
> *Lucretia rocks away*

I finish it off with Lucretia rocking because I picture an old granny woman, but because she's this gypsy up there in this attic, she doesn't care about anything.

TORNADO OF SOULS

While I obsessively listened to news about pop stuff like "Forever Your Girl," the new single from the Paula Abdul album that people claimed she didn't actually sing, "Tornado of Souls" came out of my immense pain over the end of my six-year relationship with my fiancée, Diana, while I was in rehab at the Beverly Hills Medical Center. My disease was so rampant and was ruining everything I loved, and everyone. Especially the girl I wanted to marry. In the end, we never really could connect. We could get along for periods of time, but we would always end up fighting. I believe we cared about each other a lot, but for whatever reason, we couldn't definitively hook up. It came to me—we were always safer in the eye of the tornado. I don't know why we came up with that saying, but that was what it was.

> *This morning I made the call*
> *The one that ends it all*
> *Hanging up, I wanted to cry*
> *But dammit, this well's gone dry*
> *Not for the money, not for the fame*
> *Not for the power, just no more games*

The song came from the deep regret over my breakup with Diana, even though guitarist Chris Poland had a hand in some of the later verses and someone else took a stab at the Timbuk 3 song, "The Future's So Bright, I Gotta Wear Shades." It was basically a letter that I wrote to Diana because I couldn't break up if I tried, even though I wanted to.

> *But now I'm safe in the eye of the tornado*
> *I can't replace the lies that let a thousand days go*
> *No more living trapped inside*
> *In her way I'll surely die*
> *In the eye of the tornado, blow me away*

DAWN PATROL

David Ellefson wrote this bass line. A simple little riff that didn't impress me at all at first. I kind of thought it was lame, to tell the truth, but it stayed in my head. Then, after waking one morning, having watched the night before the Jean-Claude Van Damme movie *Time*

Cop, and having a crazy dream about it, I scribbled down the lyrics to "Dawn Patrol." I told Ellefson, "Play me that riff again."

Coming to the end of *Rust in Peace,* I hadn't realized that Ellefson didn't have any writing on the album, but that had led to serious disagreements in the past. On a lot of the records, there has been one track with everybody credited as songwriter so that everybody had a share in the publishing.

He played me the lick again, and I arranged it for the demo. I started talking over the track, acting like this psycho from the future, like in the movie, and at the end where I say we spend our lives as moles, that was me distorting my voice in a twisted little knot. I had this crazy image I drew from the scene in *The Deer Hunter,* where rats trapped under a helmet gnaw at a wounded soldier's stomach, and in *1984,* with cages on people's faces and rats in front of their faces. The thought of being chewed up by rats—or any kind of wild animal, for that matter—can drive you insane. It's not something I'm afraid will happen to me, but the image in my mind is irresistibly gnarly. The song basically is my interpretation of Megadeth in the future and these people who were in authority.

RUST IN PEACE . . . POLARIS

When Metallica first started, we did a lot of cruising up and down Pacific Coast Highway, Hetfield, Lars, and me. We would drive from Orange County to Huntington Beach because that was where all the partying was. That was where all my friends were. I had gone to Marina High School in Huntington Beach. I would hitchhike up there all the time. That was where I first got my appetite for playing music at the kegger parties. We would go from party to party, drink, get blasted, and watch people play. There was something about live music that thrilled me. When the lights in the house went out and the tiny red lights on the amps gleamed in the dark at those house parties, I was captivated.

Before I joined Metallica, even before my first band called Panic, there was only a drummer named Dave Harmon and me. Dave had a drum set that I would hop on and play. That was where the drum beat for "Rust in Peace" came from and, if you listen to the drum beat, it is quite juvenile.

I wrote a guitar riff to match the beat, and that was the beginning of my jazz-influenced guitar playing. I had to make it follow that rhythm, and I used special notation that was my first shot at intricate songwriting. That was written even before Panic. I played the song at one of those parties, and the band at the party almost learned it. A number of years later, riding down the freeway with David Ellefson and listening to KLOS on the radio, I heard the song come back at me through the years by the same band that learned it from me all those years before. They even called their band "Child Saint," which was my original title for their song. To their credit, they dropped the song after I complained.

But the song "Rust in Peace" actually started with a dream I had of cruising up and down that highway, especially that water reclamation center by Newport Beach. That building served as the central piece in the dream, and there were giant tank traps—huge metal Xs like ball and jacks children's toys. In the dream, I saw kids climbing over those tank traps in front of the water towers. Also, there were these fantastic concrete conduits that kids used for skateboarding. I pictured the skaters spiraling down these pipes where people had painted band names and other graffiti.

"Rust in Peace" is a lot about the nuclear standoff, the Cold War. At the time, we were still in a cold war. A lot of folks growing up nowadays and digging on Megadeth for the first time don't know what that was and don't know how close we were to fucking ending it all, so some of the urgency of the lyrics may be lost on them. "Polaris" is dedicated to the missile itself, the warhead, and it is a simple piece, almost nothing to it. The lyrics are redundant, kind of a pedantic rhythm, to go along with the guitar riff, hypnotic in the way that it was set up. Each time that the piece passes through the riff, it picks up another little phrase. Slowly, over the course of the number, it turns into a complex guitar singer exercise.

Those two-song combinations had become a trademark of Megadeth. In the very beginning we had "Killing Is My Business . . . And Business Is Good," and people loved that. On the next record, I wrote "Peace Sells . . . But Who's Buying?" and on the next record it was "So Far, So Good . . . So What!" It was working for us.

- TWELVE -

GETTING BACK

DAVID ELLEFSON: Preparing for the release of *Rust in Peace,* our manager Ron Laffitte was very much the behind-the-scenes playmaker—busy networking and strategically repositioning Megadeth inside of Capitol Records as well as EMI everywhere outside of North America. Slayer had brought on a new manager, Rick Sales, and Ron and Rick were plotting a package tour of Slayer and Megadeth, which was nothing new for us. We had played with Slayer all the way back to L'Amour's, a small club in Brooklyn in 1985. We have history. We were rehearsing at the Power Plant—we always kept an ongoing rehearsal thing happening during that whole time—and they talked to us about a tour for the late summer/early fall, around the September 1990 release of the album that they wanted to call "Clash of the Titans."

Dave may have even come up with that name. It was easy to use. We didn't have any trademark issues with the motion picture. We put together a great bill: Slayer and Megadeth as co-headliners; Testament, who also had a new record out called *Souls of Black;*

and Suicidal Tendencies, who had also retooled and had a new album out, *Lights, Camera, Revolution!,* more of a metal punk record and not just their Venice Beach punk. That bill was going to do mostly arenas and large halls across Europe for September and October.

Knowing this was all coming into play, in the late spring Ron sent Dave and I on a promotional tour to Europe. The first stop was Cologne, Germany, where Michael Schenker was staying at our hotel. I'd gotten to know Michael a little bit earlier that year because we were both in a similar sobriety community. He is a wonderful guy, very pleasant, and Dave and I were huge fans. The elevator doors open, and there's Michael. I introduced him to Dave. It was one of those moments where I became kind of the de facto ambassador for Megadeth. Dave could be the guarded celebrity while I was the more friendly guy—the Minnesota farm boy. That could be our dynamic at times.

DAVE MUSTAINE: When David Ellefson and I went to Europe and started doing these press conferences, we were astonished. People were blown away, almost as much as I secretly was inside. I never felt that kind of excitement from the press before, seeing people have that kind of excitement about the music—it was like a drug. It was just inebriating.

DAVID ELLEFSON: We were on our own. In each city or country, there would be a local EMI press representative who would meet us there and take us around. In the UK, it was Val Janes. She was very much a good den mother. She had worked with Iron Maiden and had a great résumé. She was a real no-bullshit woman who had no problem telling us the truth and cutting right to the core.

DAVE MUSTAINE: The local EMI press representative was different in each country. In the UK, Val Janes was not so much our publicist over there; she was our European manager. Ron Laffitte had been managing the band, but he wasn't experienced enough with the European scene, so we hired Val Janes to manage the band in Europe. Val was great when we went over there.

DAVID ELLEFSON: We had a good trip to Italy, Dave and I even going to the Leaning Tower of Pisa and the cathedral in Milan. Promo tours can be fun because the travel is easy, comfortable, first class/ business class, lavish dinners from the record company every night. You sit there all day and basically talk about yourself, your band, and your record, drink coffee, and fight jet lag. Dave and I were both sober, seeing Europe for the first time through sober, clear eyes—unlike the last time we were in Europe to play Castle Donington.

It was the first trip for me and Dave to travel alone, stay in hotel rooms, and not attack the minibar. In fact, Ron had it set up that all the hotel minibars were to be emptied out of any alcohol before our arrival to avoid any temptation. He had been studying under Tim Collins, who managed Aerosmith, learning the tricks Collins had used getting those guys sober, keeping them sober, touring them sober. And, of course, Dave and I had our counselor, John Bocanegra, back home in Los Angeles who we would call and check in with from time to time as well.

DAVE MUSTAINE: We were going to European AA meetings and those were kind of fun, but it was tough. You'd check in to your hotel room, and sometimes the minibar would have shit in it. That could be hard because you're over in Europe, far from home, and there is the craving. It's not really the getting loaded or the being loaded that is tormenting; it's the craving.

DAVID ELLEFSON: During that trip, we saw the finished artwork for the *Rust in Peace* album, and I flipped out because it said all songs were composed by Dave Mustaine. I was shocked because I had cowritten songs on the record. I was also surprised by the co-production credit, "Produced by Mike Clink and Dave Mustaine," when I had been in the studio more than Dave.

Ron Laffitte went to bat for me with Dave, and we eventually smoothed out the controversy. I needed to learn how to deal with my feelings in sobriety, how to confront my issues and deal with them. Those times in my relationship with Dave, when there have been confrontations over money and credit between me and Dave, have often been very uncomfortable. Having John Bocanegra as our counselor helped. Sometimes he would call a meeting for us to sit and talk over our problems, with him as a mediator. He helped us be open with each other, knowing it could be guided to some sort of resolution, as opposed to a couple of guys getting mad at each other.

MARTY FRIEDMAN: The main way songs were written in Megadeth was that Dave would have a riff and he would play it with me, Junior, and Nick. We would be his backup band for this riff, and while he was working out the riffs, he had the luxury of us playing it and adding whatever we did. None of that stuff was written on his own; it wasn't like he came up with a riff, an arrangement, and said here it is, learn it, go record it. It was all being created with all four of us giving his ideas life.

DAVE MUSTAINE: You can clearly see why the band started to fragment. Everyone was vying for credit. "Rust in Peace . . . Polaris" was written back when I was in Panic, as was "N2RHQ," which, with two words changed and a new title, would become "Hangar 18," yet these guys are convinced they wrote those songs. The demos were done; the songs were written. The worst part for them is the proof of what little they accomplished on their own.

MARTY FRIEDMAN: To not get writing credit for that, I believed at the time, was unfair because when you are the only name listed as writer on the song, that implies that you came up with the song, you wrote the whole song yourself, and people played it and recorded it the way you wrote it. But that was not the case. He had the luxury of hearing these riffs being born in front of him and changed and worked on and arranged with the three of us around him at all times.

DAVE MUSTAINE: Uh-huh.

MARTY FRIEDMAN: But I was happy to be there in the first place and was not going to make waves. I had absolutely nothing to do with the establishment of Megadeth, the first three albums, all of the work that they did, all of the dues that they paid, all of whatever it took to get to where they got. In a sense, I was reaping the benefits of that without contributing, so I thought that was kind of the trade-off. So I was happy to work with Dave writing these riffs and not get credit for it. But as far as the actual songwriting goes, I feel like a bigger part of the process than what you see with the names.

DAVE MUSTAINE: Just a few short chapters ago, Marty was singing my praises about how I had these songs written when he came. These songs were written over time, some even from back when I was in Panic. If you go back and check the reissues, you will see that there are demo tapes of Chris Poland playing with me and the band. Marty actually has very similar guitar solos to what I asked Chris Poland to put down.

I put those demos on the reissues to give Chris some cred, but he ended up suing me, and that door was nailed shut after that stunt.

The band had this stupid idea that if I was working on a riff, that if they were in the same room as me, that they were entitled to songwriting credit. That started with Nick. He said he was entitled to songwriting credits on any of the songs that I was playing if he was standing in the same room, he didn't even need to be at his drum set. It's just crazy. As far as being in the same room, they might as well send a check to the people on the television I had in the room.

DAVID ELLEFSON: We came home from Europe and went right straight into rehearsals and started preparing the live show for the record.

GETTING BACK

DAVE MUSTAINE: Marty needed to learn the back catalog. Once we had Marty in the band, we had that band vibe again. Chuck and Jeff were great guys and terrific players, but we never felt like a band. It wasn't one of those things where you would let someone drink off your beer. But with Nick and Marty, there was something magic when we went out with those guys. That was super exciting. We were starting to feel like a band, and it was starting to show. When we went places, and the four of us showed up together, it was no longer Dave Mustaine, David Ellefson, and two other dudes. We used to be the two Daves. Now we were a band.

DAVID ELLEFSON: It was about that time that we got word that, upon our return to the USA, we were going to support Judas Priest on the band's Painkiller tour, which was a groundbreaking record for that band. Dave and Judas Priest vocalist Rob Halford were going to shoot a cover for a Japanese magazine. We went down to Studio Instrument Rentals on Sunset in Hollywood to meet Rob where Priest was shooting a video for *Painkiller*—and meeting Rob was a huge moment because I was a massive Judas Priest fan. *Unleashed in the East* had been a defining, game-changing record in my trajectory into heavy metal. After Boston and Kiss and Van Halen and a lot of American rock, when I saw *Unleashed in the East,* I finally knew what real heavy metal was. As a big fan, it was cool to meet him and start the relationship between us as touring bands.

DAVE MUSTAINE: When I saw him, I was really impressed because the kid in me was like, "This is Rob Halford." I loved seeing Glenn Tipton because of the guitar player in me, but, as a fan of Judas Priest, meeting Rob Halford was the deal. I had to go to another building to go do a photoshoot with him. I was wearing a kickboxing shirt and he had this full-length leather coat with chrome washers attached to it all the way down—so metal. Priest was one of the first truly metal bands that I listened to. In fact, I was listening to the *Sad Wings of Destiny* album in Diamond Bar, California, when I was living with my sister and her husband, who was the chief of police in Stanton, California, when he walked in the room and slapped me in the face. He heard Halford; he freaked. So, it was interesting to meet the guy that I got smacked in the face for.

DAVID ELLEFSON: Also during our preparation for the tour, we shot the "Holy Wars" video at an airplane hangar over at the Van Nuys airport. The reason we have our shirts off in the video isn't to look like a bunch of studs; it's because it was broiling in there on a hot summer day and we were sweating so bad. I was going to the gym, but when I got sober, I probably weighed about a hundred and eighty-five pounds and was badly overweight. I was working hard, training three or four days a week, going to the gym, eating well, and really trying to trim down, but I still looked a little pudgy in the video, so they stretched the film to make me look thinner. They say they did that with Ann Wilson of Heart in a video that was popular at that time.

DAVE MUSTAINE: We wanted to do the video in an old hangar, get inside, and just kick ass onstage and play around with cages, chains, and metal parts. By the time we got through the first take, my shirt was absolutely ruined. The wardrobe girl couldn't dry my shirt in time for a second take. I was in shape because I had been kickboxing with Benny the Jet. I didn't have love handles. I asked the guys how they felt. David Ellefson said he was cool with it. He looked great. Marty killed me. "You're all that, Dad," he said.

DAVID ELLEFSON: Before we went to Europe, after we filmed the "Holy Wars" video, we did a five-date warmup tour around Southern California. These were clubs, theaters, small places where we could get the band loose, figure out our set list, get the crew engaged, and start the machine working. And those were great. I still have friends to this day that talk about those shows. We were meticulous about everything, running through all the details of the songs and the sets. There was a lot of excitement because we were building something new and the possibilities seemed endless because we were clean, we had good management, we were a tightknit team. We were four brothers who really thought the same. There was total transparency in everybody's lives. It was not a one-man show. It wasn't Dave and three side guys. We were a four-piece band.

MARTY FRIEDMAN: The shows were great. The band was on fire and so was the audience. It was like nothing I'd ever done before. I had been in a lot of bands and done a lot of shows, and big shows, too, but I never saw such a violent positive reaction to any of the shows that I had ever done. I had played good shows and great shows, but when we did these warmup shows in California, this was something different. The audience was deafening. The crowd went completely ape shit. Everything we did was blowing them away, and I knew that this was a band. This was the way it should be. My ears were ringing after the shows. We proved that these four people had a chemistry. We were locked and loaded. It didn't feel like there were any weak links in the chain; it felt completely natural. We went out there and did it and it wasn't like we needed to fix this or fix that. Everything worked. What do we do next? It was good chemistry.

DAVE MUSTAINE: That was magnificent. We finally got to play together in public and it went down like a dream. We knew instinctively where one another was going to be onstage. We anticipated each other like telepathy. It was like hockey players exactly envisioning the carom off the boards. You could lean back and one of the other guys would be right there. You would run to the mic and someone would be standing right beside you singing background vocals. We were like birds in formation. This is the last time the band had any real chemistry. Every lineup that came after, David Ellefson grew more bitter and it became clear that something very bad was on the horizon.

THIRTEEN

RUST ON THE ROAD

DAVID ELLEFSON: When we went to Europe to start the Clash of the Titans tour, several important things were different. One was that we had tightened and cleaned up our stage. All our amplifiers were behind cloth screens we had built. With the giant backdrop that reflected the cover of the *Rust in Peace* album, the set looked really big. Knowing we were going to be playing the biggest arenas in Europe and coming home to the Judas Priest tour, we built a set that was economical, easy to move, but had an immense look. We moved over to Bradshaw pedal boards for Dave and Marty and kept them onstage. They could punch their own guitar solos and effects with their gear. Megadeth had always been a high-tech, advanced-technology band for metal. Unlike the grunge rock era that would follow us, which was all about Electro-Harmonix, outboard gear, all the pedal boards and such, we saw ourselves as a performance band, and that sort of mechanical technology needed to be off the deck. We made this intentional move to polish up the stage and the look of the band.

During the tour, obviously we maintained mandatory sobriety, hotel room minibars cleaned out upon our arrival and such, but we also worked out a lot, especially Dave and I. Nick was already fit. Marty was naturally skinny. But Dave and I were very much into the fitness routine, as well as hitting some twelve-step meetings while we traveled.

DAVE MUSTAINE: The Clash of the Titans tour was fun and super successful, but we got off to a rocky start. We were in Los Angeles and going to do a photo shoot for *Rolling Stone,* who were considering giving us the cover. It was supposed to be me, Tom Araya from Slayer, Chuck Billy from Testament, and Mike Muir from Suicidal Tendencies. It was going to be either a centerfold or a cover. Mike Muir decided not to show up, and I got livid because I knew that our shot for the cover or the centerfold was gone. I said something about it in the press and he didn't like it, but I didn't care. We started talking about each other, back and forth in the press, and it made me sad because I dug Suicidal Tendencies. He told one journalist in Europe that I may be a kickboxer, but he was a gangbanger and people would pay more money to see us fight than play music.

I had one of my senseis with me helping me continue to train on tour because I was going for my black belt in Ukidokan. I called up my main sensei, Benny "the Jet" Urquidez, and asked him what to do. He said, "Just go up to him, Dave, and be straight, give him the Doberman glare, and tell him this isn't good for business and if he wants, you guys can settle it when you get home at the Jet Center," our dojo and kickboxing center. I sought out Muir backstage. I held my breath, went over, and said that to him. He looked up at me. I thought, "Oh, no, here it comes." But he took me by surprise. "You know what, Mustaine?" he said. "I've got a lot of respect for you because you're trying to live sober." He told me about a friend with a drug problem and how he respected my coming up to him, willing to get it on. And I thought, "Oh, thank god." We became friends.

MARTY FRIEDMAN: I thought touring Europe was going to be great because there would be lots of chicks everywhere, but the only girl action I got was on the plane going to that tour, not during the tour. On the plane from LA to London, there was this gorgeous girl from Turkey and things happened on the plane. But when we got to Europe with the Clash of the Titans tour, the audience was like 99.9 percent dudes and there was no rock star debauchery. That was kind of a letdown after I got my hopes up.

The shows themselves were fantastic. It was a great lineup, all the bands were in a strong period in their careers, and it was all new to me, because, although I'd been in lots of bands before, I had never been on a tour with a bunch of superbands, let alone belong to one of the superbands. I had to learn to carry myself in a different way. I needed to practice being more aloof, which was new to me. You've got to carry yourself in a way that befits the image of the band. All the bands were great and it was not really a competition, but everybody was definitely trying to be top dog. We believed we were, but sometimes I would go out and watch Slayer and wonder. Slayer had this demonic magic that filled the room with this wonderful, evil sound that I wished we had a little bit more of, maybe making them ever so slightly more captivating than us on some nights. But on other nights, we were simply so on fire that no matter how menacing they were, it didn't matter because our band was kicking into high gear.

DAVE MUSTAINE: At one show, I walked underneath a curtain and up the riser to the stairs on the stage and ran my face right into a lighting truss. The European press decided that Chuck Billy from Testament must have hit me in the face. A lot of rumors were going around about us all wanting to fight, but I ran right square into this lighting truss. I had a piece of meat hanging out of my nose between my eyes about the size of a piece of a pencil eraser, and I got some Nu Skin, squirted it on the meat, and stuffed the flesh back in the hole in between my eyes. It burned like a motherfucker. You would never know that happened except when I get sunburned, a red spot shows up. It's not like I look like a Hindu woman or anything, but, in the beginning, it could be sensitive to the sun. Everybody was going, "Chuck Billy must have hit him." Yeah, right. I was very clumsy. That was all that was.

DAVID ELLEFSON: The final date of Europe was at the old Wembley Arena in London, which was a big finish. It was great to play the legendary venues. We debuted the band in London on the Peace Sells tour at the Hammersmith Odeon. Our last show in England had been Castle Donington. On the Clash of the Titans tour, we had played the Birmingham NEC the night before Wembley, so we played some big shows. Dave invited vocalist Sean Harris of Diamond Head to sing a song. He did "It's Electric" with us on the encore, before we closed with the Sex Pistols song "Anarchy in the

UK." We flew home and within a few days, we headed to Canada to start the Painkiller tour with Judas Priest.

The Painkiller tour started on the eastern side of Canada, worked all the way across Canada, five or six shows at least, and then dropped down into Seattle. We played Vancouver on Halloween. The tour wrapped up right before Christmas. We went back out with Judas Priest for another three-week kind of tertiary East Coast tour in January 1991, where we played places like Poughkeepsie, New York, and that kind of stuff. But it was good.

DAVE MUSTAINE: As the tour went along, we got closer to the Judas Priest guys. On the tour, we held a food drive—we gave out two hundred backstage passes every night to fans that would give ten pounds of nonperishable, fit-for-human-consumption food. They could bring ten pounds of green beans and get a backstage pass to do this meet and greet. We were doing the first one when Halford walked up and gave me this Bart Simpson key fob. He had heard me say I dug *The Simpsons* and handed me this little gift in front of everybody. This was when the Simpsons were still part of *The Tracey Ullman Show* and didn't have their own series yet. The next day, I got to the venue and there were Bart Simpson socks on the dresser in my dressing room. The next day, there was a Simpsons poster on the door. The next day it was a Bart phone, and I told Rob this has to stop—I don't need all this Bart shit and people are going to talk. That was a fun tour.

DAVID ELLEFSON: We all got along well. I became pretty good friends with Priest guitarist K. K. Downing. Rob Halford would give Dave presents every day, and it was open knowledge that Rob was gay. He found out that Dave was into Bart Simpson, so Rob Halford would come in every day and give him some Bart Simpson gift, a telephone, a pair of socks. It was laughingly uncomfortable. And Rob, being the wonderful guy that he is, I'm sure it was just a gesture of friendship. But it was pretty funny.

MARTY FRIEDMAN: Every metalhead loves Priest and to be on tour with them was really a dream come true, and behind one of their best albums as well. They were extremely friendly, hanging out with us, watching us from the stage. Unlike Europe, there were plenty of chicks all over the place and we were like Mötley Crüe or something. For me, that was always a big part of being in a band and don't let anybody fool you otherwise. Especially when you're first starting to get your taste of big shows. It was all arenas and Intercontinental Hotels, Hyatts, and Four Seasons, and it was a much more pleasant experience off the stage than Clash of the Titans in Europe had been, but onstage we were seriously jelling as a band. Our set list was shorter because we were supporting; we were playing an hour at the most. The tour was a total blast and it kind of got us farther in America than we might have been before. Everybody was loving this Priest—the band was on a big comeback—and Megadeth had this great new album, *Rust in Peace*. The shows were all really good, the band was tight, and we were just a lean, mean killing machine.

DAVE MUSTAINE: We got our first four-star review in *Rolling Stone* and, in fact, the writer, Robert Palmer, came out on the road with us for a while. He played his flute all night long; he would sit in the front of the bus and play his flute while we were trying to get some sleep in the back.

DAVID ELLEFSON: We were regulars on the MTV Headbangers Ball. The European music press was all over the story. "The new sober Megadeth," went the headlines. We were bold and forthright about that, put it right out there. This is a new day, it's a new Megadeth, a new band, a new record, a new lineup, and we're coming in hot, ready to melt faces.

The band was incredible. It was the first time that we really looked and thought like brothers, like a band. We listened to similar music. Marty had this theory that you either liked Zeppelin and Aerosmith or you liked Kiss and Sabbath, and Dave and Nick were more the Zeppelin/Aerosmith guys, while me and Marty were Kiss/Sabbath. It was an especially good time for us. We were a good-looking bunch of guys in our band, trim and in good shape, especially for a heavy metal band. With our videos on MTV, the girls came out. They were at our shows, which led to a lot of other extracurricular activity.

After I got sober, I was really upside down financially. I had not paid my taxes because I'd used all my money to buy drugs. I owed the IRS about $70,000, which may as well have been $7 million to me. Our new business manager made an arrangement that some of my earnings every week would go toward paying that down. My credit cards were torn up and I had some outstanding credit card bills. Dave had loaned me $5,000 from a Metallica royalty check to help cover some expenses for me. I owed a previous manager from the *So Far, So Good . . . So What!* days $5,000. I had wreckage.

I went on the Rust in Peace tour with no credit cards. Band salaries were $500 a week, plus $15 per day per diem in Europe, which doesn't buy much. We kept Marty Friedman's guitar tech, Tony DeLeonardo, who came with him the day of his audition, on the payroll, and he was making $750 a week. Our crew was getting paid more than the band. But everything was slowly coming together in my life.

DAVE MUSTAINE: I felt like we had caught up to not only Anthrax and Slayer but also Metallica. And if not catching up to those three guys, we might have even passed a few of them in terms of where we stood in the pecking order of the big four. That stuff was super important at the time. We were all vying for position. I thought this album was incredibly important to our history and our place with the other three bands that made up the big four.

DAVID ELLEFSON: We went to film the "Hangar 18" video because we needed another single. The "Holy Wars" single had played itself out through Clash of the Titans in Europe and the Judas Priest tour. We had been touring for some time. The band was tight. We looked good. We sounded good. We went into the Water and Power Plant in San Pedro and filmed. It was a pretty expensive video; we had prosthetics, we had actors, we had aliens, we had all this stuff. The final scene showed a cart pulling four canisters, an echo of the cover of *Rust in Peace,* with each one carrying a band member. We were supposed to have our eyes open with contact lenses in, looking like we were dead. I've had good eyesight my whole life. I've never worn glasses and I couldn't get the contact lenses in. We tried and tried, but I simply couldn't do it. We decided to have every other person with their eyes closed. Dave and Nick had their eyes open with contacts—Nick wore contacts in real life—and Marty and I had our eyes closed.

DAVE MUSTAINE: The "Hangar 18" video was directed by a special effect guy named Paul Boyington, and he was fantastic. He was known for his miniature set design. He built a stage that might have been more than twenty feet tall and assembled it on the edge of a square opening in the floor that was possibly 60 feet by 60 feet and maybe 80 feet down. Add the stage height to that, and I'm looking off of a 100-foot drop. He still put me right next to the edge, which made me highly nervous. If I went into some head-banging and fell off, I'm dead. They also made me wear contact lens for the final scene when the entire band is placed in cryogenic storage and you see the little miniaturized band guys being pulled away on a tram. They ladled on prosthetic makeup, which might have been somewhat corny, *Star Trek* leftovers, but this was back when record labels would spend real money on videos; "Hangar 18" had a $300,000 budget.

MARTY FRIEDMAN: We shot "Hangar 18" twice because something happened to the film, the tape got erased, or some crazy shit. It was a long video and I was not happy about doing it a second time. I was never a big fan of the fact that music videos were a necessity. I was always about going to the shows and making the shows great. At the time, I considered this a lot of extra work. It was no longer enough just being a kick-ass rock band; now we had to have visuals, too.

DAVID ELLEFSON: After that, we flew down to Rock in Rio II in Brazil in late January 1991. The headline act was Guns N' Roses, who were absolutely massive; three years earlier at Castle Donington, they were a scrubby up-and-coming band from Hollywood, and now here they were three years later, the Rolling Stones or something. Also on the bill was Judas Priest, Queensrÿche, and the Brazilian metal band Sepultura. The promoters put some pop band named Labao or something on after Sepultura, right before us, and they got booed off the stage.

MARTY FRIEDMAN: MTV gave us the star treatment, and hotel hanging and poolside partying were crazy fun, a party-like atmosphere with a lot of big bands. A lot of people at the concert. It was one of those things where you can't see the end of people. You can't see the last row. You can't see where the venue ends. As far as your eyes can see, people were going ape shit.

DAVE MUSTAINE: I was down there, I was sober, and I was with the band. We had a lot of the Guns N' Roses guys helping us on our show and it was a big-ass show, some 140,000 people—that was the first time we did that and it was pretty scary. We had heard that two people died before we took the stage. One was shot trying to sneak a fan through the fence and he was shot by an off-duty police officer. The problem was he had killed an off-duty fireman trying to sneak someone in. The other person died falling off the stadium decks.

RUST ON THE ROAD

MARTY FRIEDMAN: We decided to fit as many songs into our set as we could, so we played them faster, as fast as we could. We figured if we raised all the tempos by ten or fifteen beats, we could fit in another song. That's the spirit of a high school band and I loved that. They were like guys I would have been in a band in high school with because we all had that same spirit. It was like, "I get it, yeah, let's do that." I remember playing the shit really fast, faster than it already was, but it came off like we had all this nervous energy and it was perfect.

FOURTEEN

HAWAII

DAVID ELLEFSON: After Rock in Rio, we came home and did our first live television performance on the *Arsenio Hall Show,* where we played "Hangar 18," which was cool. It was late-night TV. And then right after that performance, we went right to the LAX airport and flew down to New Zealand and started a three-week New Zealand, Australia, and Japan tour, our first time in Australia, by the way, and finished that swing with the three shows at a little club called Pink's Garage in Honolulu.

DAVE MUSTAINE: The *Arsenio Hall* thing was cool because he got us. He said, "This group busts your brains." He was this hip black dude with a Hollywood TV show, so to get his endorsement certainly wasn't expected. And it was great to get his affirmation.

MARTY FRIEDMAN: Everybody knew that I had a big thing about Japan and Japanese women, and they never let me hear the end of it all the way up until Japan. Japan was the last part of that tour, and every day in Australia people were busting my balls about what was going to happen in Japan. I had been there once before with my previous band, which was just absolutely insane, so I knew that if I was coming with Megadeth, it would be even more insane. And it was. It was fantastic in every possible way. The shows were great. In Japan, crowds were about half guys and half girls, so you can only imagine the extracurricular activities. I also picked up with many great musical friendships that I had started the first time I went to Japan with my band Cacophony. I made new friendships with people in the music business, journalists, photographers, all kinds of people. It was everything a successful tour of Japan should be, musically, personally, everything.

DAVID ELLEFSON: In Hawaii, Dave proposed to Pam, and, two days later, he had his wedding. We all stood up in the wedding party with him. John Bocanegra was his best man.

DAVE MUSTAINE: Before we left Japan for Hawaii, one of the last things I did was buy a killer strand of pearls in this locals-only shopping district the Toshiba EMI guy took me to. I couldn't get her out of my mind. When I thought about Pam, I was feeling a feeling that I'd never felt from any of the other girls. When I got to Hawaii, I called my business manager and asked him to buy a pear-shaped diamond—I had heard Pam talking about pear-shaped diamonds—and told him to bring it to me in Hawaii. I invited my manager, his secretary, my sponsor, my three sisters, Pam's stepdad and mom and her brother. I asked John Bocanegra to be my best man. I thought it would be cool to have a bank robber as my best man. Pam knew nothing about any of this.

PAM MUSTAINE: He broke up with me before he went out on tour, and I understood the psychology of that. I get it, but I'm a principles person, and broken up means broken up. I told him I would move out at the end of the month and we could go on with our lives. During that month he would call, but I never picked up the phone. I let it go to voice mail until the last day of the month. When he called after midnight and I heard him leaving a message, yelling, "Where the hell are you?" I picked up and told him, "We're broken up, remember? It really isn't your business anymore." He said, "I've been trying to get ahold of you. I've been out here on the road and realized I can't live without you. I want to see you. Will you meet me in Hawaii?"

I met him in Hawaii. I didn't even know what this was, but I had never been to Hawaii, so I thought I would go along and see. When he got to the hotel and knocked on my door, I had just gotten out of the shower and was still wet. "What are you doing the next few days?" he asked.

I started going red, heat was going up my leg and I was getting mad. "What do you mean, what am I doing the next few days? You're the one who asked me to come out here."

I was starting to get hot, and he quickly interrupted me. "Will you marry me?" he said.

DAVE MUSTAINE: I went into the hotel room where I was staying with her, and she had just gotten out of the shower, a towel wrapped around her. I knew that the ring was coming, I knew that the business manager was coming, I knew that all the parents and all the family and all the guests and everybody were coming, so I asked her, "What are you doing Tuesday?" She said, "I'm going to be with you; what do you think?" I said, "Do you want to get married?" At that point, it was game on.

PAM MUSTAINE: I didn't even know what to think. It was like a pin got pulled. I had to catch up to what he said. I knew I loved him—I didn't want to love him, but I loved him. I was not expecting that at all. I never thought of getting married. I was in a totally different mindset and never wanted to depend on someone; it scared the hell out of me. I used to train Friesian draft horses, and you need to know what you're looking at or you can really get hurt. You learn to look for the signs, so I was always able to see into whatever it was I was dealing with. I've trained horses my whole life, horses have taught me to know what I'm looking at. If a horse doesn't think well, it doesn't matter what kind of talent you see or what that one thing is you want out of it, you're not going to be able to access it. But Dave's really intelligent and has such an amazing heart, he's so intuitive with the human spirit—Dave had such depth it was hard to put into words. . . .

If you know anything about life, you know some things only come along once in a lifetime. I knew it when I saw it. It was hard to deny, and through that "aha moment," I said yes. I had two days to find a dress. We had to get married in Hawaii because he was still in the middle of a tour. We would have the reception a month later, back home, when he got off tour.

DAVE MUSTAINE: When I want to make something happen, I make it happen. We had to find a priest, we had to do some bloodwork stuff, and we also had to find a tuxedo and a wedding gown for Pam. In Hawaii, the majority of the wedding dresses were not her size or her shape. Don't get me wrong. There's a lot of beautiful people in Hawaii, but they simply didn't come in the same shape as Pam. I ended up with a silvery, shiny tuxedo that made me look like I was going to a disco, not getting married. My legs looked like two giant sticks of Wrigley's gum.

My business manager showed up from the mainland and he had the ring. My sponsor showed up. We went out to a strip club for my bachelor party. It was totally lame. I was sober at the time and drinking near-beers, and I looked at the side of the near-beer bottle and it contained half a percent of alcohol. I started to do the math: How many of these do you have to drink to be equal to one beer? I figured you would need to drink twelve of these to equal one beer, so if I drank twenty-four that would be equal to two beers—that should give me a little buzz, but I should get a catheter and make it easy on myself.

We found a pastor. We got all the paperwork done, which turned out to be more complicated than I imagined. The location was a beautiful green park at the base of Punchbowl—otherwise known as Diamond Head—in Waikiki on Oahu, that famous volcano at the beginning of the TV show *Hawaii 5-0*.

PAM MUSTAINE: We got married at the base of Diamond Head. His sisters, my mom, and my ninety-something-year-old grandmother were being flown out even before he had asked me to marry him.

He had arranged all this. Even his business manager was flying out with *the ring*. I had *no clue* that all of this was going on.

DAVE MUSTAINE: When the time came to have a best man, everybody thought it was going to be Ellefson or maybe Ron Laffitte, but I went with John Bocanegra because he was such a badass. We were sitting on the beach in the brilliant Hawaiian sunshine waiting for Pam, joking around with the guys, going through my last-minute doubts, when a white limousine pulled up and out stepped Pam, looking more beautiful than I had ever seen her, more beautiful than I had ever seen anyone look. What struck me as she walked across the Hawaiian grass was it being so dark that it looked blue. That, and every time I had seen her before, she had been my girlfriend or my fiancée, but now I was seeing her for the first time as my wife, and the sight was amazing.

We said our vows, got in the car, and we went back to the hotel. As we pulled away, the first song that we heard on the radio was "The Living Years" by Mike and the Mechanics. Now that song never fails to bring a smile to my face when I hear it again.

PAM MUSTAINE: He wanted me to be able to tour, go out on the road with him, be with him, but I had a full-time career and I was really nervous about letting that go because that was my security, that was my life. My mom had said to me once, sometimes you've got to choose between something you love and something you love more in life.

FIFTEEN

BACK HOME

MARTY FRIEDMAN: We got a gold record for *Rust in Peace*. Eventually it went platinum, but when we got the first gold record for it, I thought, "This is crazy. This is the heaviest, most abrasive album of my career and now I've got a gold record? What have I been doing wrong up until now?" I thought the idea was to puss out and play commercial music and then sell records, but Megadeth comes out with its heaviest record of its career, sells records, and goes gold. What did it, I think, was the honesty. That record was what we were all meant to do. It was what we all wanted to do. It was what we all loved to do. We happened to have chemistry. All those good things came together for us.

DAVID ELLEFSON: *Rust in Peace* got us out first Grammy nomination for Best Metal Performance. The awards show was during the tour, but it was a big deal to be even nominated for a Grammy; it felt big-time. The music business was big-time at the moment. Artists like Madonna, Michael Jackson, George Michael, Janet Jackson were selling millions of records, and the industry was making hundreds of millions of dollars. It felt like a huge wave we were about to be swept up in.

You could feel Metallica, by this point, growing huge and, of course, Dave and Metallica have been tangled in some psychic space since he left the band. During that spring, we had gone to the studio to record "Go to Hell," and we were asked by Interscope Records, which was brand-new at the time, and the president was Tom Whalley, who had formerly been our West Coast A&R guy when we got signed to Capitol in 1986. He wanted us to do the title track for the new Bill and Ted movie, which they were going to call "Bill and Ted Go to Hell." We wrote the theme song, "Go to Hell." Of course, after we turned it in, they changed the name of the movie to *Bill and Ted's Bogus Journey*.

DAVE MUSTAINE: That song was for a movie that was supposed to have been called "Go to Hell," but they ended up calling it *Bill and Ted's Bogus Journey*, which infuriated me. We were in the studio when soundtrack producer Tom Whalley came in and urged us to make the song even heavier than it already was. The music didn't really change much after he came in and said that, but he asked me to make the lyrics really, really dark. I added stuff like "my only friend is a goat with 666 between his horns." And when we were done with the song, when they changed the name to the movie, it became such a burden always having to explain—we didn't want the song to be called "Go to Hell"; the movie was called "Go to Hell" and we had the title track. When the movie came out, it was kind of a bummer between where they placed the song and how long it was played. It almost felt like why bother? Why did we even do it?

DAVID ELLEFSON: But we kept the song, and in the number, we used a little prayer ("Now I lay me down to sleep, I pray the Lord my soul to keep . . . "). My wife, Julie, recited the prayer on our version. Back home in Los Angeles for a split second during spring 1991, and knowing that this song was going to be coming out as a single, driving down the 405 freeway, I was listening to KNAC, the big heavy metal rock station in Los Angeles. On comes the new Metallica song off the *Black Album* called "Enter Sandman," and it has the exact same prayer in it—"Now I lay me down to sleep, da-da-da." What are the fucking chances of that? Dave and Metallica. Obviously, there was a certain rivalry and suddenly we had new songs coming out at the same time with the same prayer in them. It undoubtedly added further fuel to the fire, however unintentional, yet there was no escaping the irony of how much we both think alike, how both bands are almost identical in their thought process. We were probably the two biggest bands in the genre at that point, and we couldn't keep out of each other's way.

Metallica was playing three nights at the Forum in Los Angeles. I looked around the arena and thought, "These were the exact same people who come to our concerts. Why are there three times as many of them here for Metallica? What's the appeal?" You could hear, obviously, they had slowed their tempos, they were more conscious of writing songs for the mainstream. You could tell—they were quite intentional. During this period of time, Metallica made no mistakes. Every move they made was dead on the money. Marty and I would often talk about how they always hit the mark, and, as much as sometimes Dave would make comments about Metallica, Marty pointed out that the big guy never talks about the little guy, but it's easy for the little guy to throw rocks at the big guy. Marty would have these wise observations from time to time. I took note of that.

DAVE MUSTAINE: One of the coolest things that was happening was watching the band get a new level of jet stream. We came out of the studio with a record that was way different from what was expected of us after *So Far, So Good . . . So What!*. The new album, *Rust in Peace*, elevated us. We almost felt entitled. People knew this was a much leaner, meaner Megadeth than they'd ever seen. I felt that we played better than everyone else. I didn't think that I sang as good as a couple of the guys, but I certainly thought that our band was the best out of all four of us. When *Rust in Peace* came out, it was almost like sticking a knife in the ground with Metallica. On tour with Slayer and Anthrax, we could gauge how much we were going up in popularity. I may have thought our band was the best, but Slayer was a formidable foe. Days we headlined the Clash of the Titans show, we were like kings of the world. The next night, when we were the openers, I felt like a peasant. The energy changed backstage and in the front of the house from night to night, depending on who was headlining. We had three of the big four right there, so it could get thick.

PAM MUSTAINE: I had never seen Dave play with his band. I knew nothing about that part of his life. Even when I dated him, he never played heavy metal music around me, so I didn't know that side of him. I was *just* finding out who the man was, aside from the music. He was intelligent, and that interested me along with him being intriguing and kind. His music was not even part of our beginning. We got to know each other aside from the music and what he did. When I first saw him play, it didn't make sense because I didn't know who that was up there. He was so different, *but* he is an amazing man with incredible talents, not only the ones people get to see, like the music. He's also a sensitive and truly talented man of great depth and heart. Never had I met a man with such capacity.

We went to Europe straight from the wedding in Hawaii. I had never been on the road with him. It wasn't what I thought. They weren't all crazy and drugged out—even though there was plenty of that going on, but *they weren't insane*. Where you might have thought it would be dangerous all the time, it was a surprisingly sensitive group with a lot of kind people in it. After that, I stayed on tour with him. I gave up my career because he had said he wanted me to come with him. If my mom didn't say what she did, I probably wouldn't have gone, but it was a big step for me because I just had a huge fear of depending on someone. But after we got married, all those fears went away, and we were together all the time on tour.

MARTY FRIEDMAN: At this point, we were a gleaming, polished machine. The gigs were always great. When you're that good every night, not much stands out because you go in and do your job. One thing about Megadeth—regardless of what might happen off the stage, once we hit the stage, it was killer. We loved playing together, had great chemistry, and everybody had their quarter of the diamond nailed.

DAVID ELLEFSON: Our support band in Europe always seemed to be The Almighty—we did have the same agent—but this time in spring 1991 a band we had never heard of called Alice In Chains was on the bill. We walked into the venue—the Volkshaus in Zürich, Switzerland—and Marty and I looked at the day sheet, saw the lineup, and laughed out loud at the name of the band, Alice In Chains. What kind of a stupid name is that? But we were down in our dressing room later when they went on and could hear them from the stage; they sounded pretty heavy. We went upstairs to check them out and were blown away. They looked like a bunch of lumberjacks who just crawled out of the woods and got up onstage, but they had a vibe. They were cool. They were confident. And they had a new sound.

We immediately phoned home to Ron Laffitte and told him we wanted Alice In Chains to be the opening band on the American leg of Clash of the Titans tour that summer. We were planning a three-way co-headline with Slayer and Anthrax, rotating who would close the show each night, but we needed an opening act. Scott Ian loved Alice In Chains, so the Slayer guys got on board, and they became our opening act on that tour.

- SIXTEEN -

CLASH IN THE USA

DAVE MUSTAINE: The Clash of the Titans made its way across America during the summertime and the crowds partied in their summer gear. We played all these sheds and outdoor venues and everybody wore tank tops and shorts. Girls were in bathing suits. It was a full-on party. People were having an amazing time. Anthrax, Megadeth, and Slayer always played in that order. We would rotate headliners every night, so the first night it would be Anthrax, Megadeth, and Slayer; the next night would be Megadeth, Slayer, and Anthrax. The third night would be Slayer, Anthrax, Megadeth. The audience never knew who was going to headline any particular night (unless they had figured out the formula). We felt great, but Slayer kept us on our toes. We let the chips fall where they may because it was like we were falling upwards with everything we did. Success kept coming to us by the wheelbarrows.

DAVID ELLEFSON: We finished up the Clash of the Titans playing all across the United States, and that was big. We played the biggest arenas, big amphitheaters and coliseums—Madison Square Garden, the Starplex in Dallas, all the big stuff. You could feel the groundswell *Rust in Peace* was producing. While we were on the Clash of the Titans tour, we filmed the "Go to Hell" video in Chicago with the same guys who made the "Holy Wars" video.

MARTY FRIEDMAN: "Go to Hell" was the first Megadeth song where I was credited as cowriter. We were getting along great and we were collaborating and kind of feeling each other out musically, making more use of each person's strong points. Megadeth is definitely known for being Dave Mustaine's band, and Dave is Megadeth. He has a huge imprint on what Megadeth sounds like, and Dave was smart to use what he has in his arsenal to make the best Megadeth possible. He was definitely giving me a lot more freedom than you would expect for a new guy in a band—a lot of musical freedom, a lot of musical responsibility—and drawing that out of me. "Go to Hell" was a great song but a terrible video. I had a lot of free time during the video shoot in Chicago waiting for my stage call, and Chicago is a city that I had cultivated on many fronts, even before Megadeth. I managed to have some fun. As a band, we were on fire. It was a good period of time because we proved that we could write together, make music together, and cohabitate together—a very enjoyable, musically productive period of time.

DAVE MUSTAINE: I was in New York when Ron Laffitte called and told me John Bocanegra was dead. He had done an intervention on this Persian guy and found his Persian heroin stash—all $3,000 worth of it. John's new wife, who he had married in the program, immediately claimed he died of sleep apnea, although nobody believed her. You know what they say in AA when you get in relationships with newcomers—the odds are good, but the goods are odd. I went to the funeral home and the family was fighting with one another, trying to keep his wife out of the funeral. I somehow managed to get myself involved in this bullshit and as soon as the funeral was over, I was out of there. When the coroner's report came out, it showed that the guy had two puncture wounds in his left arm. What happened was he didn't die from sleep apnea. He did a taste of the Persian, hole number one; then he shot up again, hole number two; then he died. And that was the end of John Bocanegra.

In the AA Big Book, it says something about reservations and that men who have reservations and think that someday they can drink like normal people are like men that have lost their legs. They never grow new ones. Dudes who think that one day they will be able to pick back up where they left off are delusional. I heard all the clichés—while I was in the meeting my disease was out in the parking lot doing pushups—and yeah, that's true, but Bocanegra was kidding himself all along. We were driving one day in his car and he told me to reach under the dashboard. I slid my hand under the dashboard and there was a fucking syringe. The guy's got a syringe underneath his dashboard. He never said, "One day I'm going to be able to use again," but by having the syringe, it sure the fuck meant that he thought one day he would. That's what the Big Book meant by reservations.

It was sobering in the truest sense of the word. Not that I needed a reminder that this shit, like they say at meetings, is cunning, baffling, and powerful. There but for the grace of God . . .

DAVID ELLEFSON: As we went through the Clash of the Titans tour, I could feel the tides changing. Queensrÿche had a big record called *Empire*. Metallica's *Black Album* was about to be released. That made Metallica huge. The hair-band thing was kind of stalling. Right before going out on the Clash of the Titans, and after getting excited about Alice In Chains, the drop tunings and everything, I heard Nirvana on the radio and I was like, "Who the fuck is this?" It may not be cool for heavy metal guys to sing Nirvana's praises, because ultimately the grunge movement destroyed the heavy metal and thrash metal, but I loved it. It had great punk-rock energy. I could tell a change was coming and there was a new generation on the way.

DAVE MUSTAINE: Alice In Chains jumped off the bill on Clash of the Titans because their album simply exploded. They had a hit song called "Would," their first single, that quickly vaulted the band beyond opening act status. I was excited for them, but it's never fun when someone leaves a tour, because there's always upset people and some kind of headache.

DAVID ELLEFSON: Alice In Chains had come out, Nirvana's *Nevermind* had dropped, Pearl Jam's *Ten* was coming out, and it was definitely a new shift. While we were on the Clash of the Titans tour, we were writing songs. We were writing new Megadeth songs every day. We always had backstage some amplifiers and a small drum kit, and every day when we would show up at the venue, rather than hanging out with Anthrax and Slayer, we'd come in like a military team, go straight into our dressing room, and start working on writing songs.

DAVE MUSTAINE: That's a habit that we've had pretty much since the very beginning; we've always played new songs on the road, or a little piece of them, give them a little test drive. Backstage we will be writing and work it out during sound check. For me, that's a good way to tell what songs are like. There can be magic inside a venue when you play a song.

DAVID ELLEFSON: "Foreclosure of a Dream" was a song that Dave asked me to write the lyrics. We were backstage on the Judas Priest tour in St. Paul, Minnesota, when Dave picked up his guitar and actually wrote that riff, which I found ironic. The title came from the trip where I brought Dave back to the farm where I grew up in 1986. After we recorded the *Peace Sells* record, we were on our way to New York to sign with a major label, the farming crisis was in full swing, and that was the title of a TV show we were watching, *Foreclosure of a Dream*. That stuck with us.

The night that Dave started writing that riff, my parents were at the show. It really had this Minnesota, Midwest feel. I was reading a book by Robert Heinlein, a science fiction writer, called *Farmer in the Sky*, and Dave asked me to write the lyrics. I used that book as a bit of a sounding board and I wrote the lyrics. I would get together with Dave almost daily, go over the lyrics, and he would create the melody. It became a collaborative thing as we moved into what would become the *Countdown to Extinction* record.

Every day, you would have girls and other backstage activity, but we became increasingly focused on writing the new album. We would visit each other's hotel rooms, share ideas, and collaborate on things. I walked into Nick's room and, knowing he was writing a song about canned hunts and people who hunt animals that are caged that they kill for the pelt, I told him I had just watched a TV show called "Countdown to Extinction" and thought that might be a good idea for him. "Dude, that's fucking perfect," he said, and that helped him complete the song.

DAVE MUSTAINE: Nick wrote lyrics and the title for "Countdown to Extinction," which he got from a *Time* magazine story. I saw the magazine with my own two eyes. He handed them to me much the same way that David Ellefson had handed me his lyrics for "Foreclosure of a Dream." It was a garbled mess.

DAVID ELLEFSON: The mind-set within Megadeth was that the next album had to step up our game and be ready to go. Metallica had carved the path. They showed that a scrungy little thrash-metal band could go to number one, sell millions of records, and change the world. We looked around. Anthrax didn't have the melodic perspective. Slayer was too much of a one-trick pony. We knew inside of Megadeth we had everything we needed, especially with Marty—he brought a lot of melody—and the energy of Nick. We were ready for our close-up.

CLASH IN THE USA

DAVE MUSTAINE: The best thing about Clash of the Titans was that we were breaking down barriers and playing places that had never seen bands like Slayer, Megadeth, and Anthrax before.

DAVID ELLEFSON: We finished at Lakeland, Florida. We recorded that show live. I think Slayer put out a live album from there, but I don't know that we did anything with it. Then we did a short, ten-day tour of clubs, routing us back home to California. The night after Lakeland, we played in Jacksonville, Florida, where our old drummer Gar Samuelson lived. Dave and I had not seen Gar since we fired him from the band in 1987. He came to the show and I was excited to see him. Only saw him briefly, but that was the last time Dave and I ever saw him. He died a few years later.

We worked our way across the United States, and once we got back home, went into the EMI SBK recording studio, which had moved from the building that it was in when we did the *Rust in Peace* demos, where Ron Laffitte also had an office. Now it had moved next to Le Dome, a popular, high-end restaurant/nightclub on Sunset Strip right by the Sunset Plaza. We recorded the songs that we had written on the road, a handful of tracks like "Foreclosure of a Dream," "New World Order," "Ashes in Your Mouth," and "Millennium of the Blind," which we demoed but never released until we re-recorded them on the *Megadeth 13* album in 2013. We came out of the Clash of the Titans tour with tracks that were even more metal for the *Countdown to Extinction* record.

I would say that coming off the road and putting together the first round of demos for *Countdown to Extinction,* that was the end of the *Rust in Peace* cycle.

- SEVENTEEN -

RUST REUNION

DAVE MUSTAINE: The first time I tried to reunite the *Rust in Peace* lineup was after I injured my arm and disbanded the band in 2002. I hadn't played guitar in seventeen months. I fell asleep on my arm and the doctors I saw at first told me I would be lucky to get back 80 percent use of my arm. I misheard them and said, "I will get back 80 percent of my playing again?" The doctor said, "Son, you won't be playing guitar ever again, and I meant 80 percent use of your arm."

They didn't know who they were talking to.

I went home, told everybody I was retiring, and started with a physical therapist, Nathan Koch, and this brilliant Indian doctor, Raj Singh, in Scottsdale, Arizona. They also gave me this crazy metal contraption like from *The Terminator* that I had to wear on my left hand, with rubber bands tied to a cross-piece that pulled my fingertips back, while my objective was to make my hand into a fist. All the muscles across the top of my left forearm had atrophied. I had spent seventeen months doing exercises with this thing, going for electroshock, all sorts of treatment. I was going to the gym and doing weight training, but I needed to balance my body by lifting the same weight on each side. The most I could lift with one side was two pounds. Do you know what color a two-pound weight is? It's fucking pink. I would have to go to the gym, and having all my meathead friends see me lifting two pink dumbbells was so lame.

After seventeen months of all that physical therapy, I was asked to play a benefit. One of the guys who used to work for the band had died and left his wife and child with nothing. Alice Cooper was putting the show together. I sat in at the benefit in a Phoenix nightclub, even though I could barely play more than thirty seconds of music at a time; I got the bug to play again.

I called up Nick and told him I wanted to put the band back together. He was ready to play, he said. Next, I talked with David Ellefson, who was intent on knowing all there was to know about finances. And Marty, same thing; he was not going forward with anything unless he knew how much money was involved, how much marketing, what the promotion was, what the songs were. Basically, that killed the idea of a full-on reunion, although I did ask Nick to come to Phoenix and return to Megadeth anyway. He was a mess from the moment he showed up. His drum tech had allegedly left the back door to his moving van open after stowing his gear and his drum set fell out piece by piece across the desert, from North Hollywood, California, to Phoenix, Arizona. I was told this by a session drummer in Nashville, who is very talented and who had zero reason to make this up.

The drum tech quickly proved to be a personality problem we couldn't surmount, and I had to send him home after a brief trial. We had already hired guitarist Glen Drover, now that the reunion was not panning out with David and Marty. Glen had recommended that his brother Shawn could work as Nick's tech, and while we had Nick and Shawn on speakerphone, Nick said to Shawn, "I don't even wanna fucking know you." Glen walked out, told me that either Nick left or he was quitting. Nick made a fool out of himself and lost the gig with that idiotic statement.

That was the first reunion attempt, and, after that, I decided to let sleeping dogs lie.

DAVID ELLEFSON: When I came back into the band in 2010, we did the twentieth anniversary of *Rust in Peace* tour. Megadeth and Slayer were supposed to go out on a tour called American Carnage, but Slayer bassist Tom Araya injured his neck and needed surgery. Instead, Megadeth planned a one-month twentieth-anniversary Rust in Peace tour in March of 2010. Anniversary tours were starting to be popular, and Megadeth had never done one. Of course, *Rust in Peace* was the seminal record, the fan favorite.

Meanwhile, James LoMenzo, the band's bass player, and Dave had been having difficulties and he was soon to depart the band. At the same time, the big four shows with Metallica, Megadeth, Slayer, and Anthrax were announced for the summer of 2010, and I was strongly yearning to get back into the band. I never planned on being out of the band, but after the reunion attempt in 2004 fell apart because of disagreements over business with Dave and his management team at the time, Dave and I did not see eye to eye and I ended up not coming back in the band. We dissolved our business interests, but it was never really meant in the universe that Dave and I wouldn't be in Megadeth together.

DAVE MUSTAINE: I stopped in Phoenix on a layover and called David Ellefson out of the blue. He had sued me for $18.5 million and lost. I felt compelled in my heart to have dinner with him and spend time with him because I loved him, even though he made this incredible mistake and constantly said all these terrible things about me. When I met him, the first thing that came out of his mouth was "That was the stupidest thing I ever did in my life to sue you and I'm so sorry." I told him, "I forgive you," and everything melted away. We started off again.

DAVID ELLEFSON: Drummer Shawn Drover was a big Megadeth fan, even before he joined the band. He and Dave's guitar tech, Willie Gee, bent Dave's ear about getting me back in the band, especially for this Rust in Peace anniversary tour. Shawn Drover arranged a phone call between Dave and I. We got on the phone and spoke for no more than two minutes. Any disagreements we had disappeared. I threw some basses in my car, drove from Phoenix to San Diego, and rehearsed with the band the same day I arrived. Essentially, that day I agreed to rejoin the band. The next day, I cut a track for Guitar Hero, the last one they did, a song called "Sudden Death."

That Monday, February 8, we made the announcement that I was back in Megadeth. The Rust in Peace tour started the next month. No Nick and no Marty. At this point, we hadn't even held a discussion of them being back in the band. We did that tour to great fanfare, so much so that the fans and the promoters saw the significance. We filmed the last show at the Hollywood Palladium for a DVD. It was a triumphant return for me and Dave to be working together again, like a real reunion. We continued that tour the rest of the year around the world, doing pretty much the twentieth-anniversary tour all the way. The band was really good; Chris Broderick on guitar, Shawn Drover on drums, me, and Dave.

DAVE MUSTAINE: When Shawn Drover was the drummer in Megadeth, he lobbied me hard to get David Ellefson back in the band. David and I still hadn't come to terms on our issues yet. But Shawn was a true Megadeth fan, and he put his place in the history of the band in front of his paycheck. With David back in the band, we were thinking we would bring back Marty, too. Nobody had said anything to our guitarist Chris Broderick, but Chris wasn't stupid. We were waiting for the Iron Maiden tour and we hadn't talked to Marty yet, but when Bruce Dickinson got tongue cancer, the Iron Maiden tour was off. Management told Shawn Drover and Chris Broderick the tour was off and they would need to find work for about a year. They ended up quitting very shortly after that. It was done in public, and they never told David or I, which I thought was tacky and lacking character, but that's okay. They did what they had to do to deal with their feelings at the time. If I would have been told what they had been told, I would have probably been way more upset. But once those two guys left, it was back down to me and Ellefson again. The Lone Ranger and Tonto.

DAVID ELLEFSON: We were on tour with Iron Maiden in fall 2013, seven shows across the country. Pam and Dave were looking to buy a home in Austin, Texas. Pam was standing next to me on the side of the stage watching Iron Maiden, and she commented on how popular these guys were. I told her they've had the same manager their whole career, they've never had any issues with drugs, they really carved a clean path, and that is why they are successful. They never tried to be hipsters. They never cut their hair or tried to be the flavor of the day. They are just Iron fuckin' Maiden, a dyed-in-the-wool metal band, and the fans trust and believe in them. Pam took that in. "I wonder what it would be like if we got Ron Laffitte back and put Marty and Nick back together," she said. That was the day the wheels started turning.

Ron was working now for a big-time management company. I could see Ron was getting the bug to want to manage us again. He even said he would make a great manager for Megadeth. It wasn't necessarily a bad idea. We had history. At one point, he had been a terrific manager for Megadeth. The *Rust in Peace* success would have never happened without him.

So the wheels were in motion. Twenty years later, by the end of 2013, our latest manager had been fired, and Ron Laffitte was hired.

DAVE MUSTAINE: Ellefson said, "Let's hit up Nick and Marty again," and I said, "You know what? It's just so out of control every time we ask to get these guys back in the band. What they need to be happy to come back is so unreal." I didn't like the idea. Plus, things ended so terribly with Ron the first time, I knew it would happen again. My family pleaded with me to give Ron another chance, and going sixty days without him returning my phone call and speaking to him, resulting in me firing him a second time, I realized I wasted another year of my life.

DAVID ELLEFSON: When I came back to the band in 2010, a lot of people hit me up, glad to see me back in the band, especially in Los Angeles. I heard from Andy Somers, our agent who helped build the band back in the early days, and our old manager Ron Laffitte. Around when we did the *Rust in Peace* show in Hollywood in 2010, Ron and I got together and had coffee. He told me how he un-became Megadeth's manager, a story I did not know. In 1994, he had taken this position working for Elektra Records, largely to oversee the Metallica catalog, who were selling 25 percent of all the records at the label. Ron took the job, although he never intended to not be Megadeth's manager.

There had been some pretty heavy drug relapses in 1993, which crumbled our trajectory. We never really did get that chance again. We had successes and stayed in the game, but that one chance to ring the bell went away in 1993 when Dave had a major relapse. Japan was canceled; we got thrown off the Aerosmith tour. We had an opportunity with Pantera that we couldn't seize because we had agreed to this Aerosmith tour. Metallica wanted us to stay on tour with them in Europe, but we had to be back to go out with Aerosmith, and then we ended up getting thrown off the Aerosmith tour because of comments that Dave had made. We probably should never have been out with Aerosmith. It was a long tour and the whole reason we were even put on it was the people around the sobriety community thought in order for Dave to be sober, he needed to be on sober tours. Hence, Aerosmith. That was a bad strategic move that should have never happened, period. Either you're going to stay clean or you're not. It doesn't matter what tour you're on.

Laffitte, like all of us, was deflated, but we went into the *Youthanasia* album the next year. We were nearing the end of our tour cycle in Spain, and our publicist sent us a clipping out of *Hits Magazine* that said Ron Laffitte had been hired as head of West Coast operations for Elektra Records. That came as big news to us. We had heard nothing about this before. Dave flipped out. It was never communicated to us that Ron was going to keep his management company. Suddenly, the Ron Laffitte era ended and we needed new management. That's how the Laffitte thing had ended the first time.

Except it wasn't big news to me. I knew he was up to something. One thing is for sure, if you're gonna be a liar, be a good one. He was lying constantly at the end, and I started looking for new management. How anyone can think he could do that job, manage us, *and* the Cult is one delusional motherfucker.

Dave's son Justis had taken a job as an intern with our management company, and Justis has good sensibilities. He saw the value of getting Nick and Marty back in the band and trying a *Rust in Peace* reunion. Justis didn't quite understand the complex emotional equation for Dave and me. He was looking at it from a management perspective. Dave and I resisted.

As soon as I came back to the band, this reunion idea had been bound to come around. My idea was to do it the way Kiss did, which was to have Drover and Broderick cool out on the sidelines, pay them a stipend to sit tight, and give this thing with Nick and Marty a try; it's as likely to not work. Give them some cash to hang out for three to six months. If it works, we make the decision then, and we all move on; if it doesn't, we come back and be Megadeth again with Chris and Shawn. That was not how Laffitte handled it. Laffitte tried to scare them off and push them away. By cutting their salaries, he basically forced them to walk away.

I needed to make ends meet, so I had taken a gig for a thing called the Metal All Stars. The promoter eventually got busted by the FBI for fraud surrounding these all-star tours, advertising people that weren't going to be on the bill and such. After our first day of rehearsal, I was back at the hotel when Dave called.

Dave called me in Bolivia and said, "Justis thinks we should try to get Nick and Marty back in the band." What did I think? I told him we need to find out if Marty even wants to and we need to know if Nick can even play anymore. When we fired the guy in 1998, he was messed up on drugs and couldn't play. We needed to get in a room with Nick and see if he could still play.

DAVE MUSTAINE: Justis went to hang out with Nick and saw Nick had a giant scar on his right arm. Nick had an accident with a circular saw. He was kind of a Renaissance man and had a thing about doing construction. Nick almost lost his arm because of that. David Ellefson drove him down from Los Angeles to Fallbrook, where my home studio was, to rehearse. Marty was still in Japan, but we knew we didn't need to rehearse with Marty. Nick came down and we played the first track, and it was kind of okay, but Nick kept flipping the parts upside down. By the end of the second track, he was exhausted.

DAVID ELLEFSON: Dave and Pam were going to be at their house in Fallbrook, California, in early December, and I arranged a rehearsal room in LA for Nick and I to jam, tighten him up, and check him out, before we brought Dave in. We were under pressure from management, who wanted to announce the *Rust in Peace* reunion. Nobody at management level seemed to be paying attention. What we got in 2014 from Ron Laffitte's management was not the hungry young heavy metal fan in the trenches, long hair like Iron Maiden, wearing the leather jacket, on Team Megadeth he was in 1989. The Ron Laffitte we got this time was a wealthy, successful power player at the top of the music business in Hollywood. He was working for Maverick Entertainment, Madonna's company, with clients such as Madonna, U2, Pharrell Williams. Pharrell, at this time, was a regular celebrity guest for *The Voice*. The money Ron was earning in pop music was stratospheric compared to what a heavy metal band like Megadeth would be making. As big as we were, it was pocket change compared to these pop artists.

DAVE MUSTAINE: Ron had turned into a "show biz pig." He was now everything we grew up despising.

DAVID ELLEFSON: Meanwhile, the opening band for these two shows I was doing in South America was a band called Angra, featuring hot-shot lead guitar player Kiko Loureiro. He played a couple of songs with Geoff Tate from Queensrÿche, and he and I end up jamming. I went, "Holy shit, this guy's fucking good." He was an animal onstage. His playing was incredible. I started chatting with Kiko and he told me he had moved to Los Angeles and was looking for something bigger. I didn't indicate anything was going to happen with Megadeth, but I got his phone number.

I came home from South America a couple of days later. Within that week in November 2014, Shawn Drover and Chris Broderick walked out of Megadeth in the middle of the night, putting an announcement on their Facebook pages.

The first week of December, I took Nick Menza down to Dave's studio at his house in Fallbrook to try playing. He was very nervous. We played a couple songs, starting with "Killing Is My Business"—which Nick did not play on the record, yet he played it really well. Then we did "Symphony of Destruction," which is a song Nick recorded, and he didn't play it well at all. I thought it was odd that he wouldn't know his own performance. Something was off with Nick. There were moments where he seemed lucid, in the moment, sober; and then he could be spacy and aloof. I flat out asked him, "Are you loaded?" He insisted he was sober. But on the way back to the hotel, he was talking all this weird alien, "Hangar 18" stuff. I knew something was off—I could tell something's not right here.

Meanwhile, Dave was having conversations with Marty Friedman, who lived in Japan and worked a lot over there, and the next day we got together with Nick one more time at Dave's place. This time, Dave was coming and that made Nick super nervous. We had an engineer in the studio who couldn't believe Nick Menza wouldn't show up and simply annihilate the place—this was his big chance—but instead he showed up intimidated and terrified. Dave came in the studio and we ran a couple of songs. You could tell Dave was annoyed. While I think Dave and Nick generally liked each other, when it came time to make this big move, there was a lot of stress, and it was easy to see Dave was disappointed, as was I. Dave and I never looked at each other; we just looked down at the floor. We could tell. This ain't gonna work.

MARTY FRIEDMAN: I was kind of excited about doing a reunion of some sort. I do a million projects. If I find it interesting, I do it, regardless of the money. That's how I've got where I'm at, by doing a lot of things and some of them turn out better than others. Some of them are fantastic, some I wish I didn't do, but doing them always—always—leads to cooler things. When the offer came from the manager, Ron Laffitte, I paid attention because I knew he had become a big-time manager of people like Pharrell Williams, way out of the metal league. We met in Los Angeles and I was very happy to see the guys. It was fun. Great to catch up on stuff. My main thing was I'd be happy to do it, but I'm not going to take less money than I'm already making to do it.

DAVID ELLEFSON: All through the holidays, the conversations continued about the prospects of doing this. Since we were all going to be at the NAMM show in Anaheim in January 2015, we set a meeting of the five of us—all four band members and Ron. The management company arranged a dinner. I met Dave at the hotel and we rode over together. Nick and Marty showed up on their own. Marty had asked Dave if he could bring a film crew because he was filming some kind of Marty Friedman documentary, and Dave allowed the cameras, probably partially to get the whole thing captured on film so there would be some record of it.

Marty walked in with his entourage and cameras and we sat down at the table to eat. Dave was already annoyed with Ron. I don't think they said two words to each other. Nick was sulking in the corner because he knew Dave was disappointed with him. A conversation had started about money and Nick had a manager with him named Rob Bolger, a guy from New Jersey I knew, who always seemed to be trying to find his way into the music business. He said they wanted a piece of all the profits and a salary for Nick of $7,500 per week, which is almost twice as much as I was making.

Right away, Dave got upset with these ridiculous demands, especially because Nick, who had been out of the game for almost twenty years, came in asking for a piece of everything. Right away, there were hard feelings.

You could tell Marty was feeling it out. Clearly, he was happy being a rock-star guitar player in Japan, and Megadeth was part of his past, but probably not going to be part of his future. At points, Marty almost seemed to be auditioning Ron Laffitte, asking pointed questions. Ron made some comment about rock being dead, rock means nothing, and Marty shot back, "If you think rock is dead, then you don't know anything and you're an idiot." It got a little contentious between the two.

The meeting wrapped up, but not before a brief moment where we stopped talking about business and started just bullshitting. Hey, remember when we did this? Oh my god, remember all the girls? Oh my god, remember that? Remember this fucking guy? We started telling stories for the last half hour and the meeting ended pleasantly, because we were acting like old friends.

DAVE MUSTAINE: I received correspondence through separate lawyers from both Nick and Marty at separate times. One wanted almost twice money as much as David Ellefson was getting and the other one wanted more than four times as much as Ellefson. Nick wanted to be able to sell his paintings on tour—his hats, his sweatshirts. Marty wanted us to sell his merch, too. Somehow, the guys had come up with this crazy idea that Megadeth was rolling like the Stones. They wanted more than even I get. We started seeing these crazy things going back and forth about money, merchandise, and stuff like that, and it started to get weird. Nick never understood why he was no longer in Megadeth. He didn't understand the first time he was fired or the second time. By the third time, you would have thought I would have washed my hands of this guy, but to the day he died, I tried to help Nick, even though he kept saying nasty shit about me in the press.

MARTY FRIEDMAN: I'd been in Japan for more than ten years cultivating a career with solid rewards. I was making money not only for myself but also for my management and staff. My manager has been with me fifteen years. Everything was sound and solid professionally, and when the offer came up to all of a sudden join Megadeth again, as long as I would not be making less money, I was ready to go. But I was certainly not going to take a loss to join a band that, frankly, at that point, didn't seem like they had too much to offer musically. A couple of members of the band had recently quit, and musically I hadn't heard anything that they've done in a long time. I didn't know about how relevant they continued to be in the music business. It wasn't like Megadeth was on the tip of people's tongues, at least not in Japan. I had reached the point where people stopped immediately connecting me to Megadeth and were talking about the things that I had done in Japan.

I don't know why they would think that I would immediately quit everything that I was doing to go on this tour and make less money. I don't know anybody who would do that. And, to be completely honest with you, I think, had it been more of a band situation and not such a one-man, Dave Mustaine-main-man party, I might have considered doing it for a little less. But, at the end of the day, Megadeth is so much Mustaine because that's the way he engineered it. I didn't feel that kind of camaraderie, the four-man diamond, the Beatles, Kiss, Metallica. I felt like I would be going out there and tour and it was going to be Mustaine's big success. If I'm going to do that, I'm certainly not going to lose money to do that; I was doing great on my own in Japan. And that's the way I felt about that.

Money, money, money. There . . . the truth is out. And this four-man diamond stuff? Kiss was Gene and Paul, the Beatles were Paul and John, Metallica is Lars and James. Yep, money, money, money.

DAVE MUSTAINE: At the NAMM show, the writing was on the wall, even before the dinner. I was walking across the floor of the Anaheim Convention Center, making my way to my car to go to the dinner, surrounded by bodyguards and people asking for autographs. We were making our way through the mob, and Marty was walking along by himself when the security guards pushed him out of the way. I went, "Whoa, whoa, whoa," but that shows how things were, the trajectory of myself and Megadeth continuing upward, while these other guys, not so much. If anything explained why Marty would say all of these unkind comments, this kind of dynamic did. What was I supposed to do? Be upset that I was famous? That is what I love to do. It's what I live for. Some of them walked away from music, some of them simply couldn't do it anymore. Nobody left Megadeth and went on to glory like I did after leaving Metallica.

DAVID ELLEFSON: After the NAMM meeting, we pretty much let the whole thing go. The project was done. Dave changed management.

Drummer Chris Adler from Lamb of God—a big heavy metal band a generation behind us, grew up on Megadeth—approached us. He knew we were going through this transition and he also knew we were talking to Nick Menza. Dave went into the meeting with Nick, Marty, and Ron knowing he had Chris Adler in his back pocket. Two weeks later, we tapped Chris Adler for the album sessions.

Chris had recently changed management with Lamb of God and had hired 5B Artists + Media, and he convinced Dave to come aboard. When Dave told me that he signed with new management, I was relieved. These guys were real heavy metal managers. They get our music, they understand us. So that was the end of the Laffitte regime; time to move forward and be the new Megadeth now.

One of the first things Dave told new managers at 5B when he hired them was for them to find him a guitar player. They put together a short list and on the list was Kiko Loureiro, who I had just played with in November. Dave called me up, said he thinks he found the new guitar player—Kiko Loureiro. I told him I knew Kiko, had played with him in South America, and had all his contact information. I emailed Kiko and asked him to knock out a few videos of him playing Megadeth songs at home and send them back to me and Dave. In Dave's mind, Kiko was already in the band.

Less than a month after that meeting at NAMM, which was really the final nail in the coffin of everything, we had new management; a new drummer, Chris Adler, ready to play; Kiko Loureiro was in the band; and we were locked and loaded and ready to go. It was an awesome moment. By February 2015, we said goodbye *Rust in Peace*, goodbye Nick and Marty, goodbye Ron Laffitte. That was then, this is now, close the door, end of chapter, time to move forward and write new history for Megadeth.

DAVE MUSTAINE: Nick was having trouble playing, and then we thought maybe we would have Chris Adler play on the record, and Nick would play on tour, but once I started playing with Chris Adler, I made up my mind that was it, I would stick with Chris Adler, and put a pin in the reunion for the second time. We made *Dystopia* with Chris Adler and we got our first Grammy. Any hope for any future reunions came crashing to an end one year later, when Nick Menza died from heart failure onstage at the Baked Potato, a jazz club in North Hollywood.

EIGHTEEN

CODA

DAVE MUSTAINE: I'm an American success story. I have had so much bad stuff happen to me—both at my hand and at the hands of other people—where I shouldn't be successful. Hell, I shouldn't be alive. In fact, I died once. I want people to know the blood, sweat, tears, and struggle behind the music. Maybe people will understand more why this record makes them feel the way it does after they see all the emotion behind it, everything that was going on. Now they can see why the band was so volatile and the music so fraught with feeling.

My mom and dad divorced when I was four years old. When I was fifteen years old, she moved out and I was on my own. I had to learn how to take care of myself, how to fight. Consequently, I got beat up a lot, but that's what led me down this road. I don't get beat up anymore.

Everything that formed me went into that album at the time it was made. Everybody should know the incredible journey of that album's life, why I wrote the songs, how I fell in love with my bandmates, how heartbroken I was when I couldn't get it back together, and the human side of everything behind *Rust in Peace.* It was not simply the recording of an album; it was the triumph over a lifetime of adversity, a coming together of powers greater than myself, and the culmination of earthly and cosmic forces whitehot enough to forge the mighty steel of which that album is made.

DAVID ELLEFSON: When we did *So Far, So Good . . . So What!,* we were disjointed, internally and musically. And, of course, we were junkies. We were on drugs, barely keeping it together at the beginning of the cycle, clearly falling apart by the end. *Rust in Peace* was vital to planting the flag for Megadeth again. And here was this record that we wrote in our absolute darkest hour, yet recorded it stone cold sober, with amazing clarity and precision. The sober recording set in motion the operational mandate for how the rest of the campaign would go as a live touring band, the precision we had, the attention to detail we paid, and the connectivity between us. We were a team. Manager Ron Laffitte was 100 percent committed and everyone stayed sober. That gave us all hope that there was an even brighter future ahead of that.

MARTY FRIEDMAN: All great musicians have done countless projects with the equal amount of determination, equal amount of hopes, and equal amount of motivation and money, circumstances, and luck—all those things. We all are doing the best we can all the time and looking back to ask why this one was different than all others is somewhat useless. I can't tell you what it was about *Rust in Peace*. I know it was not a preconceived record made in the boardroom by a bunch of people plotting success; it was four guys doing what we did best and what we did most naturally, and that's all it was. It really sounds like what we sounded like. There were no effects.

A lot of the Megadeth things that we did afterwards were good, but they have a lot of bells and whistles that I could have done without—weird voices, unusual intros, and strange things that clouded up the music. On *Rust in Peace,* there was not even reverb on that fucking record. It's just straight up four guys plugging into amps, no reverb on the drums. It was dry—bone dry—and it worked.

DAVE MUSTAINE: If Marty had problems with all the production, thirty years later is not the time to bring it up. He sure didn't say a peep to me.

MARTY FRIEDMAN: I think all of our stuff was great and I think we did the best we could on every record and believed in everything equally. As much as *Rust in Peace* worked, we believed all of the records that we made together were equally as good if not better than *Rust in Peace* or else we wouldn't have released them. We never went into a mixing session being done and said, "Wow, this isn't as good as our last couple records, but let's put it out anyway." Believe me, at the time *Risk* was done, we all felt exactly the same way we did after *Rust in Peace.* You always give a thousand percent and you never know how it's going to fall. I've worked so much harder on other projects, before and since, that have gotten way, way less recognition. Who's to say what makes a classic?

MIKE CLINK: I couldn't have predicted the success of *Rust in Peace* when the songs were six, seven minutes long, with all those time changes and vocal melodies that were not super-poppy. Radio at that time was not playing records like that. They weren't playing Megadeth records. I knew it was a great record, but I had no clue what it would sell. Not an inkling. I knew that the record was great and that the band was amazing. Even though I pieced the record together, they were amazing players. To watch Mustaine play those rhythm parts with such accuracy, or to hear Nick Menza play all those songs with the time changes, Junior, picking as fast as he would pick, and Marty, so effortlessly melodic—they boggled my mind.

DAVID ELLEFSON: It's that one album fans always want to hear. We have two landmark albums in our catalog, *Rust in Peace* and *Peace Sells*. Those are the two. *Peace Sells* was our first record on Capitol Records. Of course, the title track was a hit on MTV, the first big mainstream look that the world got of Megadeth. *Rust in Peace*, in its weird way, was sort of a rebirthing of Megadeth. And the next big look the world would get of Megadeth. *Rust in Peace* is an album that we wrote in our darkest days and then recorded in our brightest days with our brightest future. It set the stage for everything that was going to happen from the day it was released, really, up to this day now and beyond.

CODA

I think when you're a band and you have an album with such fan acclaim, it doesn't matter what the critics say. Especially not in heavy metal. The only thing that matters is what the fans say. When you have an album like *Rust in Peace*, you essentially have a calling card forever. If you make four or five or ten more bad albums after that, you will always have that one album that will forever endear you to your fans.

Fortunately, Megadeth continued to have an extremely high output of great-quality material, and even the nineties, which were a very treacherous time for heavy metal, with Seattle music coming in, the Nu-metal movement coming in, the whole FM radio rock movement that happened by the late nineties, Megadeth trying to somehow navigate those waters making records like *Youthanasia, Cryptic Writings,* and even the *Risk* album. Even though I didn't participate in reinventing the band during the mid-to-late 2000s with *United Abominations* and *End Game,* they were definitely very well-thought-out, strategic moves by Dave. It was ironic that I would turn back up in 2010 on the downbeat of the twentieth-anniversary Rust in Peace tour.

DAVE MUSTAINE: Going back over all these details of what the people involved remember, some of it has changed my recollection of the way *Rust in Peace* went down. Some of it has only confirmed to me that they are still wrong to this day. Remembering those times was a bittersweet experience. As great as it was to go over all the triumphs, all the different players, and other folks who played a part, and see what made this record happen, it was also equally painful to hear things like Ellefson saying if a lot of drugs didn't

189

screw up our friendship, a little bit of sobriety did. True enough. We don't hang out anymore. And while I know life goes on, I, too, miss those days when we were close friends as well as musical brothers-in-arms.

I always tried to make Megadeth a four-piece group, but in addition to some of the big lineups, there were others that weren't worth mentioning. The public voted by record sales. None of us completely understood the bond we forged making *Rust in Peace* together. As haphazard and rocky as the path may have been, something beautiful, something lasting came out of all that madness and catastrophe. There have been many Megadeths, but something about that *Rust in Peace* quartet lingers in everybody's minds—the musicians', the fans', mine. I tried hard to make that reunion happen. More than once. But it was not to be. What we had was like electricity, and how can you put that back in the bottle?

It was great to go back and look at all this stuff, but all it did, really, was get me even more excited to make the next record. No telling what all these memories have stirred up in the depths of my creativity, below where words can reach, where all great music is born. We haven't started recording this thing. We finished the book in time to start the new record, another cycle of rebirth for the band. We will see where all this goes because Megadeth is always wearing shades and looking into the sun. Here's to another thirty years.

PHOTO CREDITS

All photographs are by Gene Kirkland except as noted below.

Photograph of Dave Mustaine and Andy Sommers courtesy of Andy Sommers

Photograph of Bob Nalbandian courtesy of Bob Nalbandian

Photograph of Chuck Behler courtesy of Brian Kniaz

Photograph of Dave Mustaine, Tony Lettieri, and Romell courtesy of Tony Lettieri

Photograph of Pam Mustaine courtesy of Pam Mustaine

Photograph of Mustaine wedding party in Hawaii courtesy of Dave and Pam Mustaine

Photograph of Randy Kertz courtesy of Randy Kertz